Happy Cooking!!

Mary Kay

The NON-INTIMIDATING COOKBOOK for people intimidated by COOKING

"Food is not about impressing people. It's about making them feel comfortable."

- Ina Garten

The NON-INTIMIDATING COOKBOOK for people intimidated by COOKING

Mary Kay Callahan

ISBN: 979-8-218-74142-6
Book Cover Design: Brien Spanier
Designer: Emily Lanctot
Food Stylist: Lisa Valley

Engine light is on, Unexpected huge bill, Trips to the ER, Horrible e-mail from the boss, Gray hairs, Saw a spider in the kitchen, Kids with the stomach flu, Bad report cards, Dog poops on couch, Broken snowblower during a blizzard, A giant sliver, Late for work, New water heater went out, Neighbor lady complains about your kids in her yard, Last minute babysitter cancellation, Kid didn't make the team, Airplane tickets booked for wrong date, Just got phone scammed, Toilet overflows,

A LOT OF THINGS ARE SCARY. COOKING FOR FAMILY AND FRIENDS DOESN'T HAVE TO BE

Giant zit appeared out of nowhere, Flat tire, Old jeans don't fit anymore, Horrible haircut, Just got letter from IRS, Lost credit card, Keys fell in garbage disposal, Kids are carsick and you forgot the bucket, Speeding ticket, Incessant dog barking in your neighborhood, Swimsuit shopping, Boring presentations, Need new furnace, Coworker talks too much, Bad coach for your kid's team, Expired license tabs, Forgot to set the garbage can out for pick up

Feeding a Family Can Be Messy But it Can Also Be Fun

We've all been there. The in-laws are coming over for Thanksgiving and you've never cooked a turkey before. You forgot you are supposed to bring an appetizer to a party that starts in an hour. Your new neighbors just moved in and you want to welcome them with something you baked but you have no idea where to start. Your friend just had a baby and you want to bring her and her family a meal but what do you make? The list goes on and on. Being overwhelmed and intimidated in the kitchen is totally normal and exactly why I decided to write a cookbook that is a little different than the bazillion cookbooks out there. One that not only shares amazing recipes by days of the week, but recipes that I have curated over the past thirty plus years (yes, I am old!), that will give you confidence and more importantly, joy in your cooking journey. My recipes with less meal prep are earlier in the week on Mondays and Tuesdays. As the week progresses, I include side recommendations to pair with main dishes. These recipes may require a few more steps but are easy to follow and they are NOT intimidating. I promise! Once the weekend arrives, I have brunch recipes, app recipes, entrees with side recommendations for when hosting a dinner party, cooking for a crowd and yes, desserts which are perfect any day of the week! Lastly, I included a holiday section with some tips and great recipes to navigate your holiday meals and create lasting memories!

My Inspirations For Putting A Good Meal On The Table

Hi, I'm Mary Kay!

Welcome to my cookbook. Many of the recipes in this book are from my mom, Mary Jo Chapman Thank you, Mom! My mom passed at the age of 94 while I was working on this project. She was my inspiration for creating this cookbook and I am dedicating it to her. My mom loved to cook for family and friends. She hosted Christmas Day at her house annually until she was 91! Gourmet meals no less! My mom's love for putting a delicious meal on the table daily for her family (seven kids plus my dad) when we were growing up in Iowa (I now live in Minnesota), and her love for entertaining was what instilled in me a passion for cooking and baking and ultimately, writing this cookbook. My hope is that with this cookbook as your guide, your meal times become amazing share times, memory times, laughs times and great conversation times with your family and friends, courtesy of me!

I want to thank my husband, Charlie Callahan for encouraging me to write this cookbook and for sound advice on how to get it done! Thirty-six years of marriage and not one complaint of anything I made for you! Also, I would like to thank my three kids, Molly, Charlie and Danny. How lucky am I to get to be your mom? Thank you for always being my obliging taste testers in the kitchen. I love you all.

My mom at 90 years young. My biggest cheerleader.

To you holding this cookbook in your hands, I hope you enjoy it as much as I have enjoyed creating it for you.

Happy cooking!

Table of Contents

Weekend Wonder Appetizers Cont'd

What's in Mary Kay's Kitchen?

I am sharing with you in this chapter what I strive to have on hand at all times in my kitchen. It makes cooking and baking so much easier when you feel organized in the kitchen. It stinks when you are already into baking a pan of brownies only to realize you are completely out of flour. The last thing you feel like doing is running to the grocery store right when you are ready to mix your dry and wet ingredients together. It's maddening but it happens.

This chapter serves as a guide for you to cook and bake with ease. I share what I keep in my pantry, what essential kitchen tools I recommend (beyond the basics like a wooden spoon, spatulas, measuring cups, etc), and what I stock in my freezer and refrigerator.

Now let's take a peek...

The **Gotta Haves** For Your Pantry

Basil
Dried basil is a must have at all times in your kitchen. You can use it in your soups, sauces, salads, stir fry, literally anything! Basil has a slight peppery flavor and smells so good. Plant some basil in the summertime so you have fresh basil to cook with.

Cinnamon
Popular ingredient for baking and to put on apples or in an apple salad.

Chili Powder
Key ingredient for chili and barbeque sauce.

Cumin
This spice has a slightly sweet and warm flavor. It is used in stir fry, Mexican, Mediterranean and Indian dishes.

Oregano
Popular in Italian and Mediterranean cooking but I add to soups, stews and egg dishes.

Red Pepper Flakes
If you like a little extra punch of flavor and a little heat, this is a great spice for you! I add to my eggs in the morning, stews, stir fry, roasted veggies, pasta sauces and pizza.

Paprika
Adds color and depth of flavor to soups, stews and meats.

Peppercorn
Create your own fresh black pepper with peppercorns and a good quality pepper grinder. It adds depth to any recipe.

Sage
This is a key ingredient for chicken noodle soup, roasts and stews. I love it on sweet potatoes when I am frying them up with veggies to go with my eggs for a weekend brunch!

Sea Salt
I prefer sea salt but all salts are pretty versatile. Salt is a key ingredient when cooking as it assists in building the flavor profile of your dish.

Thyme
Adds a savory flavor to pork, beef, chicken, soups and roasted veggies.

Garlic Cloves
I used to buy the minced garlic in jars but now I use only fresh garlic and I advise you to do the same. Yes, a little more work but the fresh garlic will give your dish more flavor. Store in a garlic keeper. This allows proper airflow because the garlic keeper has holes in it. This will keep garlic dry and extend the shelf life. My college friend, Sally gave me one and I will never go back to the jarred garlic!

Flour/Granulated Sugar/Brown Sugar
Always great to keep on hand. I store mine in clear plastic containers with tight fitting lids. I used to bake all the time when my kids lived at home. I still like to bake but only when my kids will be coming over, or I am baking for a friend or entertaining. Brown sugar can get rock hard if not used regularly. Keep a slice of bread in your brown sugar container to keep it soft.

Vanilla Extract
Key ingredient for baking. Splurge and buy the pure, not the imitation. Your tastebuds will thank you.

Baking Soda & Baking Powder

Boxed Yellow Cake Mix, German Chocolate Cake Mix, Evaporated Milk, Sweetened Condensed Milk, Caramel Bits, Chocolate Chips, Mini Marshmallows, Butterscotch Chips and White Chocolate Chips
Because you will be making my butterscotch marshmallow bars and caramel bars in this recipe book all of the time!

Krusteaz Boxed Cinnamon Swirl Coffee Cake
This is the best coffee cake, for real! I have made homemade coffee cakes but this boxed coffee cake is equally as good and so dang easy! I always have on hand for weekend brunches, or if having overnight guests or heading up north to a friend's cabin for the weekend. Everyone loves this coffee cake and it tastes like homemade. Shhhh...it will be our secret.

Near East Chicken Flavored Boxed Rice
I have at least three boxes of this in my pantry at all times. I do not have a rice cooker and don't feel like I need one as I love this boxed rice! It is so easy to add to an entrée for a quick weeknight meal.

Extra Virgin Olive Oil
I have a huge jug of this on hand at all times.

Red and Yellow Onions
I like to use red onions for salads, in stir fry dishes and on my hamburger. When browsing through this cookbook, you will notice, I use yellow onions in almost every main dish! It's all about layering of flavors!

Potatoes
Sweet potatoes and Yukon gold potatoes are used regularly in the Callahan house. We love sweet potatoes diced and stir fried with veggies and over easy eggs for a weekend brunch or as a side to a week day entrée. Easy to microwave and have with a grilled chicken breast. It is naturally creamy, flavorful and so healthy! Idaho potatoes are ideal for mashed potatoes or just baked with a dollop of sour cream or added to roasts and soups.

Balsamic Vinegar
This is a universal condiment that I drizzle on roasted vegetables, use as a marinade for salmon or chicken or in a homemade salad dressing.

Apple Cider Vinegar
Super healthy and used in homemade salad dressings, marinades and sauces.

Canned Black Beans
For your soup and salad recipes.

Canned Mexicorn
Because like my family and friends, you and your family and friends will be obsessed with the corn dip recipe in this book and you will need ingredients on hand at all times!

Canned Tomatoes
For chili, soup and entrée recipes.

Chipotles in Adobe Sauce
I use this a lot when I am wanting more heat in whatever I am making. Use sparingly!

Coconut Aminos
I use this in place of soy sauce as does not contain soy. It is made from the sap of a coconut palm tree. It has less sodium and you don't sacrifice any flavor by substituting this. Oh, and it does not taste like coconut!

Dried Cranberries and Almonds
Great additions to a tossed salad.

Pistachios
For homemade pesto and for sprinkling on brussel sprouts or in a tossed salad for added flavor and crunch.

Fig Jam
Great with cheese and crackers for a quick appetizer or to add to your charcuterie board.

Hot Honey
Hot honey is great on roasted vegetables, cheeses, pizza, and in sauces and marinades.

Beyond the Basic Kitchen Essentials

Grater/Zester
Ideal for salad dressings, marinades, stir fry (I grate fresh ginger in my stir fry), sauces and baking. Adding zest will elevate the flavor to cooking and baking!

Instant – Read Thermometers
Quick, easy and will calm your mind as you do not want to serve undercooked meat to family and friends. Chicken temperature should read: 165 degrees F, beef, and pork should read: 145 degrees F.

Potato Peeler
Buy a sturdy one as you will use this for not only potatoes but for cucumbers, butternut squash and carrots.

Potato Masher

Good Quality Knives & Knife Sharpener
I recommend three knives. An 8 inch chef's knife. Useful for slicing thick cuts of meat, slicing through watermelon, butternut squash, etc. A 6 inch utility knife for dicing and slicing. A 3 ½ inch paring knife for mincing garlic, hulling strawberries, peeling vegetables, etc.

Trudeau Toss and Chop Salad Tongs
A friend gave this to me for my birthday and I am obsessed! It is so great for chopping lettuce for tossed salads. No more huge leaves of lettuce hanging out of your mouth!

Lemon and Onion Storage Containers for Fridge
Keep sliced onions and lemons fresher longer in these containers.

Salad Hands
For serving and tossing salads.

Lemon Juicer
Quick and easy way to juice your lemons and leave the seeds behind.

Wave Slicer
For a fancier way to slice your veggies.

Twist & Pour Salad Dressing Container

Avoid Trips to the Store with a **Stocked** Freezer

Bread
We don't eat a lot of bread but we like to have some on hand so freezing it is perfect as then it is always there when we want it!

Chicken Breasts and Boneless Chicken Thighs
I always load up on chicken breasts (and some boneless chicken thighs), as this is the meat I use the most when cooking.

Ground Beef
Whether you are going to grill burgers, make tacos or Sloppy Joes, ground beef is always good to have on hand.

Frozen Fruit
Great for smoothies and for making my recipe for frozen fruit cups.

Leftovers
Make a double batch of soup or brownies or any entrée and store for later in freezer. Can be frozen for up to 3 months!

Pork Tenderloins
These are often on sale at the grocery store so I always buy them to have on hand. My favorite pork tenderloin recipes are included in this cook book. Give them a go!

Shrimp
A large bag of uncooked large shrimp as you will be making my shrimp salsa and shrimp with rice dishes all the time!

Trader Joe's Lava Cakes and Vanilla Bean Ice Cream
These are so delicious. I always have on hand in case I am having company over and crunched on time but I want to serve a dessert.

Turkey Breast
I make both of my turkey chili recipes in this cookbook a lot so it is nice to have the turkey breast on hand when I am craving chili. I also like to serve a turkey breast for Sunday night dinners with mashed potatoes and my broccoli corn bake in the winter time. Awesome comfort food without too much hassle (especially if you buy the store bought mashed potatoes).

A Well Appointed Refrigerator Keeps **Everyone & Everything** Chill

Apples & Apple Sauce
Great as a snack, in tossed salads, or sliced to go with an entrée for an easy weeknight meal.

Better Than Bouillon Chicken Base
For soups and other recipes that call for chicken broth.

Celery
Great in soups, tossed salads, egg salads, tuna salads or just to eat as a snack when craving something crunchy or for something green as an easy side!

Butter & Eggs

Cream Cheese
Staple for many appetizers.

Dijon Mustard & Yellow Mustard
Used in marinades, salad dressing, sauces and dips.

Greek Yogurt
Great for making smoothies, and a great substitute for sour cream or mayonnaise.

Mayonnaise and Sour Cream
Key ingredients for dips and sauces.

Cottage Cheese
Excellent source of protein.

Freshly Grated Parmesan Cheese
For salads and toppings for entrees.

Red Cabbage
With a crunchy texture and mild flavor, this beauty keeps forever in the refrigerator! Great added to roasted vegetables. Excellent source of vitamins C and K.

Red Peppers
Adds a pop of color to any entrée or app. Delicious roasted, too, with olive oil and salt!

Spinach and/or Spring Salad Greens
Add spinach to your smoothies or to your scrambled eggs in the morning. Lettuce salads always pair nicely with any entrée.

Blueberries
Great for a healthy balanced diet. Use as a salad topper, in smoothies or pop in your mouth for a quick snack.

Family enjoying the holiday hard work.

Almond Milk
For smoothies.

Sriracha
Trader Joe's brand is our family favorite. Put on eggs, roasted veggies, cottage cheese, stir fry, anything! This is a hugely versatile condiment if you like a little added heat to your dishes.

Pickles
Great in egg salad, tuna salad, on burgers or as an easy side to pair with an entrée. My mom always said that you have to have something green on your plate!

Turkey Breast or Chicken Breast
I like to cook a turkey breast or a chicken breast and slice it up and keep in refrigerator. Convenient to have on hand for salads or when making soup or sandwiches, especially my turkey & cranberry wraps!

A Whole **New Way** to Think About **Meal Planning**

Weeknight Meals

Life can be nuts any time but especially during the week. You motor through the day on autopilot and fall into bed at night exhausted wondering if life is always going to be this chaotic. Looking ahead to your week and meal planning is going to make you feel organized and will lessen the burden on everything you have going on. If you plan ahead and prepare healthy and flavorful meals during the week, your family will be fueled and ready for a productive week!

Look at your week as, "Okay, I need to grind through Monday, Tuesday, Wednesday and sometimes Thursdays. If I can get a healthy meal on the table those night with leftovers one of the nights, I am almost to the weekend!" The weekends are for letting the clutch out. You may want to dine out, do carry out or make a bunch of apps and have a family game night or entertain some friends. Whatever the scenario, feel good about what you accomplished during the work week and enjoy your weekend. You earned it and you, my friend, are amazing!

Monday

"Rainy days and Mondays always get me down." Lyrics from The Carpenters. I am really dating myself here but I always think of this song on Mondays because Mondays are tough and daunting. You may be recovering from a busy weekend and if you have a family, they are too. Or you may have had a wonderfully relaxing weekend at home or traveled and now reality hits and you are back to the grind of the work week. Whatever the scenario, come Monday, you are not going to feel like doing a lot of meal prep. I am here for you! The recipes in this chapter for Monday meals are super easy to make.

Don't forget the sides! It is easy to skip the sides when making a main dish but the sides are what balances out the meal. It adds a pop of color to the plate and as a result, will be more appealing to otherwise picky eaters. Earlier in the week, keep your side dishes super simple such as: a salad in a bag from the grocery store, carrots, celery, applesauce, apples or pickles. As my mom used to say, "You need to have something green on your dinner plate!"

I came up with this recipe when my kids were little. Similar to chicken noodle soup but heartier. It is everything kid friendly and so easy and quick to make. Serve with apple sauce sprinked with cinnamon or my autumn apple salad (recipe on page 44).

Chicken Noodle Casserole

1 package 8 oz noodles (I use rotini)
1 baked rotisserie chicken, deboned and skin removed
1 can cream of chicken soup
½ t garlic powder
½ t paprika
2 T butter, melted
Cooking spray
¼ cup chicken broth
Dried or fresh parsley
Grated parmesan cheese, optional

Cook the noodles according to package directions. In an 8x8 glass dish, coat bottom of pan with cooking spray. Place noodles in pan. Shred chicken and mix chicken with the cream of chicken soup and the melted butter. Pour chicken broth over casserole. Cover with foil and place in 300 degree oven for 20 minutes. Sprinkle with parsley and parmesan cheese once removed from oven.

Serves 4

These sandwiches are great for using leftover turkey from Thanksgiving or a great summer sandwich option for a picnic in the summer. My family loves these sandwiches so I make them any time of the year!

Turkey & Cranberry Sandwich Wraps

3 lb frozen turkey breast (or left over sliced white or dark meat from whole turkey)
1 can whole berry cranberries
2 - 8 oz bricks of cream cheese, softened
8 to 10 inch flour tortillas
8 oz package provolone or swiss cheese
Romaine lettuce
8 sheets of plastic wrap or aluminum foil

If not using leftover turkey from a previously cooked turkey, cook turkey breast according to package directions. Let cool, then slice into 16 slices.

Mix cranberries and cream cheese together in a mixing bowl until well combined. Spread to your liking a good amount of this over one tortilla. May have some spread left over and store in air tight container for another time. Starting at end closest to you, layer two slices of turkey breast (may overlap), a slice of cheese and some romaine lettuce. Roll tortilla tightly starting at end with layered ingredients to other end. Cut wrap in half and place on a sheet of plastic wrap or foil and roll tightly. Refrigerate until ready to eat. Can chill in fridge for several hours.

Makes 8 Sandwich Wraps

This homemade taco seasoning is way better than store bought taco seasoning. Great on fajitas and as a dry rub for chicken breasts too! Double, triple, quadruple the seasoning and store extra in an air tight container for a later use. GF

Beef Tacos

1 lb beef
1 t olive oil
½ cup chopped onion
1 cup water
½ t ground chipotle powder
½ T cumin
½ t onion powder
½ t oregano
½ t paprika
½ T coriander
¼ t garlic powder
Salt to taste
Six corn hard shell taco shells
Toppings: shredded cheddar cheese, salsa, green onions, shredded lettuce, sour cream guacamole, jalapenos, tomatoes, cilantro

Brown the beef in a skillet with 1 t olive oil. Use a wooden spoon to break up the beef. Once the beef is browned, drain the grease and set beef aside. In same skillet, add chopped onion and sauté until tender. Add beef back to skillet and add the water and spices and bring to a boil. Once boiling, cover and reduce heat to a simmer for about 15 minutes until mixture has thickened. Fill hard shell or soft shell tacos or place on a bed of mixed greens for a taco salad.

3 Servings

This dish is similar to one I found online from A Pinch of Yum. I made some tweaks to it. Double this recipe and freeze the second batch for another time. Can be frozen for up to three months, just be sure to cool to room temp before storing in an airtight container in your freezer. Don't forget to label your container!

Easy Turkey Chili

1 cup quinoa or farro (farro not GF)
2 cups chicken broth (I use Better Than Bouillon)
3 cups water, divided
1 T olive oil
½ red or white onion, chopped
½ red pepper, chopped
2 stalks celery, chopped
2 to 3 cloves garlic, minced
2 to 3 jalapenos, minced (remove ribs and seeds, otherwise really spicy)
1 lb ground turkey
1 - 14 oz can black beans, rinsed and drained
3 T chili powder
½ t paprika
1 t cumin
½ t coriander
1 t salt
1 cup salsa
2 - 14 oz canned crushed fire roasted tomatoes
Toppings: sour cream, shredded cheddar cheese, green onions, tortilla chips

Bring chicken broth and 1 cup of water to a boil in a small saucepan. Add the quinoa or farro, cover the pot and reduce to a simmer for about 30 minutes or until all liquid is evaporated. While the quinoa is cooking, in another pot, heat the olive oil over medium high heat. Add the onions, pepper, celery and jalapenos. Saute for 1 – 2 minutes, adding garlic last minute of cooking time. Add the turkey and cook until all the meat is browned and broken apart into crumbles. Add the black beans, chili powder, cumin, salt and salsa. Simmer for a few minutes then add the tomatoes and however much of the remaining 2 cups of water you need to get the right consistency. Simmer for a few minutes while the quinoa or farro finishes cooking and then add to the rest of the ingredients. Top with your favorite toppings.

6 Servings

When my kids were in grade school, I volunteered along with other parents to cook lunch and dinner for the teachers and faculty at parent teacher conferences. This recipe was served for lunch and comes from another parent volunteer, who so kindly shared the recipes. It became an instant family favorite. Thank you, Mary N.! This dish is easy to make as all ingredients are thrown into a crockpot, including the raw chicken. Everything cooks on low for several hours and all the flavors meld together resulting in a very tasty soup with a slight kick.

Crockpot Chicken Taco Soup

1 small onion chopped
2 cans black beans (drained)
1 can corn (drained)
1 - 15 oz can tomato sauce
1 can/bottle beer
2 cans fire roasted tomatoes
3 T of my homemade taco seasoning (go to my beef tacos recipe on page 24)
or 1 pkg taco seasoning mix
About 3 chicken breasts (one pkg)
To increase heat, add crushed red pepper flakes or cayenne pepper.

Add all but chicken to crockpot and stir. Lay uncooked chicken breasts on top pressing down slightly to cover. Cook for five hours in crockpot on low heat. Remove and shred chicken, add back to soup and cook another two hours on low. Serve with tortilla chips, sour cream, cheddar cheese, avocado, cilantro etc.

8 Servings

My mom gave me this recipe when my kids were little. It is super easy, yummy and the perfect week night meal when you are short on time! Serve with mashed potatoes or rice. GF

Chicken Breasts in Orange Sauce

6 boneless chicken breasts
1 t pepper
1 t paprika
1 small can undiluted orange juice (buy frozen but let thaw for this dish)
½ t thyme
1 t rosemary
Dried or fresh parsley

Lightly sprinkle chicken breasts with pepper and paprika. Place chicken breasts in a 9x13 pan sprayed with cooking spray. Pour orange juice over chicken and sprinkle with thyme and rosemary. Bake uncovered in a 350 degree oven for 30 minutes. Once removed from oven, sprinkle parsley over chicken breasts and spoon extra sauce over breasts.

6 Servings

This is a super easy dish and you can use any veggies that float your boat. I use whatever veggies I have in my refrigerator. Red and yellow peppers, mushrooms, onions and broccoli are usually what I use for this dish. Great served over rice, quinoa or riced cauliflower. I especially like it with Trader Joe's Mexican-Style riced cauliflower. I just add at end of cooking time of veggies and cook until heated through along with the turkey and spices. Sometimes I just add the riced cauliflower and skip the veggies if I don't have them on hand or I am short on time. This recipe allows for lots of wiggle room! GF

Turkey Kielbasa and Veggie Stir Fry

One 13 oz turkey kielbasa sliced (comes precooked)
2 T extra virgin olive oil
1 red pepper, chopped
1 orange pepper, chopped
1 large onion, chopped
1 cup fresh broccoli, chopped
1 cup mushrooms
2 cloves garlic
1 jalapeno, optional
1 t oregano
Salt & pepper to taste

Heat olive oil in a sauté pan, add chopped veggies and oregano and jalapeno if using. Stir fry until cooked through, add garlic. Cook another minute or so. Slice turkey kielbasa and add to dish and heat through.

6 Servings

No Meat Monday

Simple & Delicious Non Meat Dinner Options to Kick off Your Week

I make this soup throughout the fall and winter. It is pleasing to both the eye and the palette. I made it for Halloween family and friend gatherings when my kids were little before everyone headed out to trick or treat. My neighbor and dear friend, Camille loved it so much, it became her family's Thanksgiving tradition to serve before the turkey!

Butternut squash can be a challenge to peel. Be sure to have a good quality potato peeler and that will do the trick. If you end up with extra butternut squash than what the recipe calls for, freeze the uncooked chunks for a later use. Squash can be frozen up to three months. GF

Apple Squash Soup

¼ cup butter
1 cup onion chopped
1 ⅛ cup chicken stock
1 cup salsa verde (green salsa or just regular salsa works too)
1 cup water
1 lb (about three cups) squash, pared, seeded and cut into 1 inch chunks
2 cups unpeeled tart green apples cut into 1 inch pieces
1 ½ T fresh minced rosemary or 1 ½ t dried
¼ t coriander
¼ t pepper
¼ cup toasted sliced almonds for garnish
Salt to taste

In a Dutch oven (thick walled cooking pot with a tight fitting lid), melt butter and then add onion and sauté until tender. Add stock, salsa, water, squash, apples and spices. Bring to a boil, reduce heat, cover and simmer 25 to 30 minutes or until squash is tender. Stir occasionally. Puree soup in batches in food processor or blender. When pureeing or blending, let soup cool a bit, otherwise the pressure build up from the steam could cause the soup to explode. I speak from experience and it's no fun wiping soup off your cabinets, counter top and kitchen floor. The ceiling is a challenge too! After pureeing, return soup to Dutch oven and simmer 5 to 6 minutes until thoroughly heated. Garnish with toasted almonds.

4 Servings

In the fall and winter, I am obsessed with soups, stews and chili! I came up with this recipe several years ago when I wanted to make more vegetarian meals. This chili has a kick to it and is very flavorful and filling! GF

Veggie Chili

1 T olive oil
1 large onion, chopped
3 cloves garlic, minced
2 stalks celery, chopped
2 T chili powder
½ t paprika
1 T brown sugar
1 T cumin
1 T oregano
½ t coriander
⅛ t allspice
⅛ t ground cloves
½ jalapeno pepper, seeded and chopped (optional)
1 ½ cups water or vegetable stock
1 cup red pepper, chopped
1 sweet potato peeled and diced
3 T tomato paste
1 - 14 oz can diced tomatoes, undrained
Toppings: shredded cheddar cheese, sour cream, cilantro

Heat olive oil in Dutch oven over medium heat. Add onions and celery. Cook until softened. Add garlic, spices and jalapeno and cook a few minutes longer. Add water and next four ingredients and bring to a boil. Reduce heat to a simmer and simmer for twenty-five minutes. Top with cheese, sour cream and cilantro.

4 Servings

A great recipe from the Minneapolis Star Tribune Taste section with a few tweaks from me. I don't have a lot of fish recipes but this one is a go-to!

Baja Fish Tacos

½ cup sour cream
½ cup mayonnaise
¼ cup chopped fresh cilantro plus more for garnish
3 T of my homemade taco seasoning (go to my beef tacos recipe on page 24) or a 1.25 oz store bought taco seasoning packet, divided
4 cod or other firm white fish fillets cut into 1 inch pieces
2 T olive oil
1 t lemon juice
12 - 6 inch flour tortillas, warmed
¼ head of red cabbage, shredded (about 4 cups)
2 tomatoes, chopped (about 1 ½ cups)
Lime wedges

Combine sour cream, mayo, cilantro, and 2 T taco seasoning in bowl. Combine fish, oil, lime juice and remaining taco seasoning mix in a large nonstick skillet. Cook over medium high heat, stirring frequently (about 4 to 5 minutes or until cod flakes easily when tested with a fork). Spread sour cream mixture over center of tortillas. Top with cabbage, cod, cilantro, tomatoes and a squeeze of lime juice. Use corn tortillas for GF option.

4 Servings

This recipe was inspired by a recipe from the Minneapolis Star Tribune Taste section. I made a few tweaks to it to make it my own. With the chipotle in adobe sauce and the smoked paprika, this hearty vegetarian dish, packs in a lot of flavor! GF

Smoky Sweet Potato Chili

1 T olive oil
1 cup chopped onions
½ cup diced red pepper
¼ cup chopped celery
3 cups diced sweet potatoes
2 garlic cloves
1 chipotle in adobe sauce, chopped (or ½ of chipotle if you want just a little heat)
1 T chili powder, to taste
1 t smoked paprika
2 t ground cumin, or more to taste
1 - 14.5 oz can diced tomatoes
2 cups vegetable or chicken stock
3 cups black bean, or white or navy beans, drained and rinsed
Salt and pepper to taste
Cilantro for topping (optional)
Sour cream for topping (optional)

In a large pot over medium heat, add the olive oil and then the onions, pepper and celery. Sweat veggies (cook but not until browned), then add the sweet potatoes, garlic and chipotle in adobe sauce (just the chipotle not sauce unless you want this dish to be super spicy). Add spices stirring until fragrant, about 1 to 2 minutes. Add tomatoes and stock. Bring to a boil and then turn down to simmer. Simmer for 30 minutes stirring occasionally. Check to make sure sweet potatoes are tender. Add more stock if chili is too thick. Stir in the beans and stir until heated through.

6 Servings

My sister-in-law, Laura gave me this recipe. If you like black beans, make this soup! Great source of fiber and protein. The key to thickening this soup without flour is pureeing some of the black beans before cooking it. GF

Spicy Black Bean Soup

Cooking spray
1 medium uncooked onion, chopped
4 cloves minced garlic
3 - 15 oz cans black beans, undrained, divided
½ t red pepper flakes, or to taste
1 t ground cumin
14 ½ oz chicken broth or vegetable broth
10 oz can of tomatoes with green chiles
15.25 oz can of yellow corn, drained (optional)

Coat bottom of large stockpot with cooking spray. Add onion and garlic and cook, stirring frequently until onions are soft but not brown, about 5 minutes. Place one can of beans in blender, add sautéed onion mixture, red pepper flakes and cumin. Cover and blend on high until smooth, about 30 seconds. Pour mixture back into stockpot. Place second can of beans and broth in blender and puree until smooth. Add to stockpot. Stir third can of beans (do not puree first), tomatoes and green chiles (and corn if using) into stockpot. Bring to a boil, lower heat to medium and simmer for 20 to 25 minutes.

8 Servings

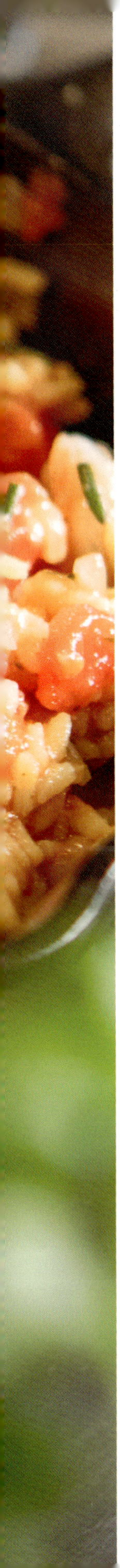

You will love the flavors of this dish and how quick and easy it is to make. You are welcome.

Shrimp and Rice

½ cup onion, chopped
⅓ cup green or red pepper, chopped
¼ cup butter
2 cloves garlic, chopped
1 - 28 oz can diced tomatoes
1 cup water
1 t dried rosemary
¼ t paprika
1 package Near East Rice Pilaf
1 pound raw frozen shrimp, thawed, rinsed and tails removed
2 T butter
Salt and pepper to taste

In a saute pan, melt butter and add onion and pepper. Saute until tender then add garlic, tomatoes, water, spices and rice. Bring to a boil and then simmer for 20 minutes or until rice is tender. In another pan, melt the 2 T butter and add the shrimp. Cook until shrimp is pink. Add cooked shrimp to rice dish last few minutes of cooking time.

2 – 3 Servings

Super hearty, healthy and flavorful. GF

Crockpot Moroccan Lentil & Chickpea Soup

1 ½ cups dry green or red lentils, rinsed and drained
1 large yellow onion
1 inch grated fresh ginger
2 cloves garlic
2 carrots, chopped
1 red bell pepper, chopped
1 yellow pepper, chopped
1 celery stalk, chopped
1 - 14 oz can diced tomatoes
4 cups chicken or veggie broth
½ cup water
1 to 2 T red harissa
2 t smoked paprika
1 t cumin
½ t coriander
¾ t cinnamon
Salt and pepper to taste
1 T fresh lemon juice
1 - 14 oz can chickpeas
½ cup cilantro

To crockpot, add the lentils, onion, ginger, garlic, carrots, pepper celery, tomatoes, chicken broth, 1 ½ cups water, harissa, and spices. Stir to combine. Cover and cook on low for 6 to 8 hours or on high 4 to 6 hours. Just before serving, stir in the lemon juice, chickpeas and cilantro. Cook soup until heated through. If soup is too thick, add more water or broth.

6 Servings

This is a basic tuna salad recipe that I elevated with the added capers. Capers give the dish a lemony tang and since soaked in brine, no need to add salt to this dish! Great served on toasted bread, a croissant, a bed of mixed greens or sliced tomatoes! GF

Tuna Salad

3 - 5 oz cans chunky light tuna in water
½ white onion, chopped
½ red pepper, chopped
¼ cup radishes, chopped
¼ cup celery
¼ cup sweet pickle relish
⅛ cup capers
1 T fresh dill weed or 1 t dried
¼ cup mayonnaise (or more if you like your tuna salad extra creamy)
Pepper to taste

Drain tuna from can and put in a mixing bowl. Pat the tuna dry with a paper towel. Add rest of ingredients and mix well. Refrigerate until ready to serve.

8 Servings

This recipe is from the first cookbook my mom gave me right after I got married. It was from a fund raiser for the Dubuque (my home town in Iowa) Symphony Orchestra. I made a few changes to the original recipe. It's the perfect healthy soup on a cold Minnesota winter's day. GF

Spinach & Lentil Soup

5 cups chicken or vegetable broth
1 cup dry lentils, rinsed and drained (any color but red makes dish most attractive!)
2 T olive oil
¾ cup chopped onions
1 rib celery, chopped
1 small red pepper, chopped
1 medium carrot, chopped
2 cloves garlic, minced
1 t thyme
1 t turmeric (optional)
8 oz canned tomato sauce
1 pound fresh spinach leaves, chopped
⅓ cup medium or hot salsa
Salt and pepper to taste

In large soup pot, bring broth to boil. Add lentils, cover and simmer for 30 minutes. In skillet over medium heat, add oil then add your veggies and spices and sweat the veggies for about 10 minutes. Add minced garlic the last minute of cooking time. Add vegetables mixture and tomato sauce to lentils. Cover and cook on low until lentils are very tender, about 20 more minutes. Add spinach, cover and cook an additional 5 minutes (may seem like a lot of spinach but it wilts quickly). Add salsa. Add salt and pepper to taste. Thin with water if you don't want a thicker consistency.

8 Servings

I love making this soup in the summertime when tomatoes are at their best. This is a chilled soup and is so flavorful and colorful. GF

Gazpacho Soup

4 large fresh tomatoes, diced
½ English cucumber, peeled and finely diced
½ cup finely diced red bell pepper
½ cup celery
¼ cup minced green onion
1 large jalapeno pepper, seeded and minced
2 cloves garlic, minced
1 t salt
½ t cumin
½ t coriander
¼ t oregano
¼ t cayenne pepper
Freshly ground pepper
1 pint cherry tomatoes
¼ cup olive oil
1 lime juiced
1 T balsamic vinegar
1 t Worcestershire sauce
3 T fresh basil or 3 t dried basil

Combine first seven ingredients into a bowl. Stir in salt, and rest of spices. In a blender, add cherry tomatoes, olive oil, lime juice, balsamic vinegar and Worcestershire sauce. Cover and puree until smooth. Add pureed mixture to tomato and cucumber mixture. Stir to combine. Cover and refrigerate at least two hours and preferably more to let flavors settle in.

4 Servings

Tuesday

You made it through Monday. Woot, woot! I included in Tuesday meals, easy side recipes that will pair well with your entrées. You are already two days into your work week! Don't even think about doing carry out. It's only Tuesday. Get that meal on the table. Be a grinder. Let's Go!!!!!

My mom gave me this recipe and it has been my son, Charlie's favorite dish since he was in first grade. This was his birthday dinner request every year growing up. It is especially good with the autumn apple salad recipe and rice. I like the Near East chicken flavored boxed rice.

Parmesan Chicken

6 boneless chicken breasts
½ cup softened butter
½ cup flour
1 t salt
1 rounded cup parmesan cheese
Dash of paprika

Mix ingredients (except the chicken) together. Separate into six sections working the mixture into balls. Can wet hands to make ingredients easier to work with. In a 9x13 baking dish sprayed with olive oil, place the chicken breasts. Cover tightly with foil. Bake in 350 degrees for 2 hrs. Remove foil last 15 minutes of baking time. Sprinkle with paprika.

6 Servings

This is my go-to recipe in the fall and winter, especially when apples are in season. It pairs wonderfully with pork and chicken and looks especially pretty served in a glass bowl. This came from a cookbook my mom gave me by the Dubuque Symphony Orchestra League. She gave it to me shortly after I got married to nudge me into getting into cooking. It worked! GF

Autumn Apple Salad

2 T lemon juice
2 T honey
2 T brown sugar (optional)
½ t cinnamon
Pinch of nutmeg
Pinch of cloves
Pinch of allspice
4 large apples, thinly sliced (I use 2 Honey Crisp and 2 Granny Smith)

In large bowl combine lemon juice, honey, brown sugar and spices. Quarter and core the apples leaving skins on. Cut each quarter into four or five slices and add to lemon juice mixture. The lemon juice will keep the apples from browning. Toss gently to coat apples. Chill until ready to serve.

6 to 8 Servings

I always double this recipe and freeze it. This is a wonderful soup to bring to a family member or friend who is ill. Awesome comfort food! Seve with some crusty bread and a salad!

Chicken Noodle Soup

1 store bought cooked rotisserie chicken or 3 cups cooked chicken, shredded
2 T olive oil
1 onion, chopped
2 carrots, peeled and diced
2 stalks celery, diced
1 - 8 oz package dried egg noodles
2 cloves garlic, minced
1 ½ t sage
1 t oregano
1 t poultry seasoning
6 cups chicken broth (I use Better Than Bouillon)
1 T parsley
Parmesan cheese for topping (optional)
Salt to taste

Debone the chicken, if using a store bought rotisserie chicken and shred the meat being careful to remove all the bones. Set chicken aside. Cook egg noodles according to package directions, drain and set aside. Sweat the veggies in a Dutch oven or sauce pan. Add minced garlic to the veggies. Next add the chicken, chicken broth and spices except parsley. Simmer on low for twenty minutes. Add the cooked noodles at the end of cooking time ending with the parsley on top. If soup is too thick, add a little water until desired consistency. Once soup is in serving bowls, sprinkle with parmesan cheese.

Other options: add broccoli florets, replace egg noodles with 7 oz cheese tortellini

6 Servings

This recipe is also from a fundraising cookbook my mom gave me (my first cookbook!) that raised money for the Dubuque Symphony Orchestra (in Iowa where I grew up). I make it regularly for my family but also for friends and neighbors going through a difficult time. Whether it is a birth of a new baby, an elderly neighbor who is too frail to cook, someone recovering from a surgery or sickness, someone mourning the loss of a loved one, whatever the situation may be, this is comfort food at its best. Serve with my autumn apple salad recipe (found on page 44). These two dishes pair so nicely together and are easy to transport if making for someone else but of course your own family is going to love it too! When preparing this meal for others, I always use aluminum disposable pans and prep everything and put baking instructions on lid. The recipient can put in their own oven, eat at their own convenience and not have to worry about washing and returning any dishes. GF

Herbed Pork Tenderloin With Oven Roasted Potatoes

⅓ cup olive oil
2 cloves garlic
½ T fresh rosemary or 1 ½ t dried
2 T minced fresh thyme or 2 t dried
½ t salt
¼ t pepper
2 whole pork tenderloins (¾ to 1 pound each)
2 lbs new potatoes, unpeeled and quartered or halved depending on size

Preheat oven to 375 degrees. In medium bowl, combine olive oil, garlic, rosemary, thyme, salt and pepper. Coat tenderloins with 3 T seasoning mixture and place in large roasting pan. Toss potatoes in remaining seasoning mixture until well coated. Arrange the potatoes around the tenderloins in pan. Roast for 45 minutes or until juices run clear. Stir potatoes about half way through roasting time. Once done roasting, remove dish from oven and let sit for 5 minutes before slicing.

4 to 6 Servings

This is a super quick and delicious week night meal that can be made ahead of time or at the last minute. Recipe was inspired from Six Sisters Stuff online. GF

Korean Beef Bowl

⅓ cup brown sugar
¼ cup coconut aminos
1 T sesame oil
½ t crushed red pepper flakes
½ t fresh ginger, minced
1 T olive oil
3 cloves garlic, minced
1 pound ground beef
½ cup chopped red pepper
3 green onions, chopped
Cooked rice

In a small bowl, whisk together brown sugar, coconut aminos, sesame oil, red pepper flakes and fresh ginger. Set aside. Heat olive oil in large skillet over medium high heat. Add red pepper and cook two minutes and then add ground beef cooking until browned. Add minced garlic last minute of cooking time. Drain off excess fat from beef. Stir in coconut aminos mixture and green onions. Cook until heated through. Serve over cooked rice. I like Near East but some of their rice is not GF. This dish is delicious with my Frozen Fruit Cups recipe on next page

4 Servings

My mom always had frozen fruit cups on hand when we would visit her and my dad when my kids were little. They loved Grandma's fruit cups! Her recipe had more sugar in it. I cut back on the sugar. This recipe is a great side dish to any entrée during the winter months when you are missing the summertime fruit. GF

Frozen Fruit Cups

½ cup sugar
1 cup water
1 - 16 oz package frozen strawberries, blueberries, raspberries or blackberries
1 - 16 oz package frozen mangoes or peaches
4 fresh bananas
1 can crushed pineapple
12 cupcake wrappers

Bring water and sugar to a boil. Let cool. Cut the still frozen strawberries and mangoes/peaches into thirds (small chunks). Cut the fresh and peeled bananas into small chunks. In large bowl, combine the fruit and cooled sugar water. Using large spoon, scoop fruit mixture into paper lined muffin tins., Place in freezer for at least 4 hours. Pop frozen fruit cups out of muffin tin and place in freezer bags in freezer until ready to serve. Let sit at room temp for 15 minutes or so before serving. Can be frozen for up to three months.

12 Servings

This pesto recipe is made with pistachios instead of pine nuts. My friend, Angela D. made it this way for a girls' cabin weekend and I was hooked!

Pesto with Pistaachios

4 cups basil, loosely packed
2 T pistachios
2 T extra virgin olive oil
¼ t salt
2 cloves garlic
½ cup grated fresh Parmesan cheese
2 t butter, softened
2 cups uncooked penne pasta

Combine first five ingredients into a food processor, process until finely minced. Place in a large bowl. Stir in cheeses and butter until well blended. Cook pasta according to package directions. Drain in colander over a bowl, reserving 3 T cooking liquid. Add pasta and reserved liquid (this reserved liquid will help pesto stick to the pasta), tossing to coat.

4 Servings

Serve this dish during the week for a quick and easy meal that does not skimp on taste! Add my parmesan salad or if short on time, Caesar salad in a bag from grocery store plus garlic bread and you have yourself a stellar meal! Extra delicious in summertime when using fresh tomatoes from your garden or the farmer's market!

Tomato Pesto Pasta with Chicken

1 cup pesto from recipe above
2 T olive oil
2 cups shredded chicken from a store bought rotisserie chicken
1 - 8 oz package mozzarella cheese
½ cup parmesan cheese
1 - 14 oz can diced tomatoes, drained
3 T fresh basil, chopped or 3 t dried

Cook pasta according to package directions. Mix pesto and olive oil with noodles and lay in a greased 9x13 glass baking dish. On top of pesto/noodles, layer chicken and tomatoes. Sprinkle both cheeses and basil over top, cover with foil and bake at 350 degrees for 30 minutes, removing foil for last 5 minutes of cooking time.

4 Servings

My mom used to make a salad similar to this. This salad pairs well with any meal but especially pasta. Add some grilled chicken for a one dish meal!

Parmesan Salad With Basil and Tomatoes

⅔ cup extra virgin olive oil
3 T lemon juice
½ t seasoned salt
1 clove garlic, mined
1 t dried basil or 1 T fresh
1 bunch green onions, chopped
1 cup cherry tomatoes, sliced in half
½ cup shredded parmesan cheese plus a little more for sprinkling on top of salad
Croutons (optional)
8 cups spring green lettuce leaves, torn (or lettuce of your choosing)

Mix first five ingredients together and put in bottom of a large bowl (preferably the one you will be serving the salad in). Add lettuce to bowl. Set tomatoes and croutons aside until ready to serve. Lettuce with dressing at bottom of bowl can be refrigerated for up to 8 hours. When ready to serve, top salad with tomatoes and croutons. Mix well making sure all dressing at bottom of glass dish is fully incorporated. Top with more parmesan cheese and if using, more croutons.

You can easily double, triple or quadruple this recipe and serve a big crowd by keeping warm in crockpots or a portable oven. This dish freezes well too! Just thaw in fridge and then heat on warm in oven, crockpot, stove top or portable oven.

Sloppy Joes

1 to 1 ½ lbs hamburger
¼ to ½ cup onion, finely chopped
½ green pepper, chopped, optional
1 clove garlic, minced
1 can tomato soup
1 ½ T vinegar
1 T sugar
1 T yellow mustard
3 T ketchup
8 to 10 hamburger buns

Brown hamburger in skillet. If using hamburger with a lot of fat, drain beef. Return back to skillet and add onions, peppers and garlic for last minute of cooking time. Continue to cook until onions are softened stirring frequently. Add rest of ingredients and reduce heat to low and simmer for 20 minutes.

Makes 8-10 sandwiches

This recipe is super easy to make and a crowd pleaser. GF

Broccoli Salad

1 head broccoli, chopped into pieces (about 6 cups)
12 slices bacon or turkey bacon cooked and crumbled
½ cup raisins (optional)
½ cup chopped pistachios
1 cup mayonnaise
¼ cup sugar
¼ cup red onion, chopped
¼ cup chopped red pepper
2 T white vinegar

Add broccoli to a pan of boiling water and cook for 4 to 5 minutes until tender. Immediately remove broccoli to an ice water bath (a bowl of ice and water big enough to hold the broccoli) to stop cooking. You don't want mushy broccoli! Drain broccoli to dry. In a large bowl, mix together remaining ingredients and add the broccoli at the end. Cover with plastic wrap and place in refrigerator for at least one hour before serving.

4 Servings

Wednesday

Hump Day! Two more days to go and then the weekend. Maybe Wednesdays are for leftovers? Leftovers were nonexistent in my household for a while. My boys, Charlie and Danny were athletes and like many adolescent boys, were growing like weeds and they could eat! Anything that was not finished during meal time was devoured before they went to bed. I always felt bad for my daughter, Molly, as she rarely got to enjoy leftovers the next day!

If leftovers are not an option, (or maybe you froze your leftovers for another time), fear not, the recipes for Wednesdays are easy, delicious and have side recipe recommendations. You're welcome.

My grandma had a recipe similar to this recipe. I have made some tweaks to it. This dish makes a great fall or winter week night meal. Serve with Carrots and Parsnips recipe on next page. GF

Pork Chops With Potatoes and Mushrooms

4 bone in pork chops
4 baking potatoes peeled and sliced length wise
1 T olive oil
1 onion, chopped
1 carton fresh mushrooms, sliced
2 cloves garlic, chopped
1 can cream of mushroom soup
½ cup chicken broth
3 T olive oil, divided
1 ½ t paprika, divided
1 ½ t dried sage, divided
½ t salt
2 t dried or 1 T fresh parsley
Pepper to taste

Preheat oven to 400 degrees. Grease a 9x13 glass baking dish. Coat pork chops with olive oil, paprika, sage and salt. Layer potatoes in dish. Saute on medium high onions in pan with remaining olive oil, add mushrooms. Cook until onions and mushrooms are softened, then add garlic and cook for one minute stirring so garlic doesn't burn. Add cream of mushroom soup, chicken broth and spices to pan. Mix ingredients together and pour over potatoes in baking dish, covering all the potatoes. Place potatoes in oven for 15 minutes. Remove from oven and turn temp to 350. Gently place pork chops over potatoes. Return to oven and cook for 30 minutes checking internal temperature of pork chops for doneness (145 degrees). Sprinkle with parsley and pepper.

4 Servings

After returning from a trip to Ireland with my husband, I was inspired to recreate a delicious dish we had at an Irish pub. The combination of parsnips and carrots with the sweetness of honey and the crunchiness of the toasted walnuts was delightful. I always crave this side dish in the winter and I like to pair it with my pork chops recipe on previous page.

Sauteed Carrots & Parsnips

1 lb carrots, peeled and sliced
1 lb parsnips, peeled and sliced
1 ½ T olive oil
2 T butter
1 T fresh rosemary or 1 t dried
1 ½ T honey
¾ cup walnuts, toasted
1 t dried parsley or 1 T fresh
Salt and pepper to taste

Heat oil in skillet. Add sliced carrots and parsnips. Sautee for about 10 to 12 minutes or until vegetable are crispy tender and a little brown around the edges. While carrots and parsnips are cooking, in a separate dry skillet, place your walnuts on medium high heat. Watch carefully so they do not burn. Stir frequently and once walnuts are a little brown and smell toasted, they are done, about five minutes. Place walnuts in skillet with the carrots and parsnips. Turn heat to low. Add butter, rosemary and honey and stir until well combined. Add salt and pepper to taste and top with parsley. Serve immediately or place in oven safe dish and keep on warm in oven.

Serves 4 to 6

My whole family loves Thai food. It is a go-to for when we want to do carry out on the weekends. Sometimes I crave it during the week and obviously healthier to make my own. I have been making this Thai dish for years and my family devours it. If you dig Thai food, this will become your favorite too! GF

Thai Chicken Stew

4 boneless chicken breasts or 12 chicken thighs
3 large Yukon potatoes, peeled and cut into chunks
3 large carrots, sliced
1 cup fresh broccoli florets, chopped
2 T olive oil
1 large white onion, chopped
1 red pepper chopped
1 to 2 tomatoes, chopped (or 1 16oz can diced tomatoes work too)
~~½ can cold water~~
1 cup water
1 - 14 oz can unsweetened coconut milk
4 T curry powder
3 T brown sugar
½ t cayenne pepper, optional
Salt and pepper to taste

Bake chicken breasts (or thighs) in 350 degree oven for 30 minutes. While chicken is baking, peel potatoes, cut into large chunks. Heat a large pot of water to a rolling boil. Add potatoes, cover and cook for 10 minutes. Next, add carrots to boiling potatoes and cook both for an additional 10 minutes. Lastly, with 3 minutes of cooking time, add broccoli. Once done cooking, drain and set aside. Cook onions, peppers in a sauté pan with olive oil for 10 minutes or until tender, adding minced garlic at the last minute of cooking. Add tomatoes, salt and pepper. Cook another five minutes. Add this mixture to pot with cooked potatoes and carrots. Add rest of ingredients to the pot and simmer for 20 minutes. Pair with Waldorf Salad on next page!

6 Servings

I like to make this salad in the fall and winter. Sometimes I tire of a tossed lettuce salad and crave something with more crunch and diversity. This is an awesome and unique salad with dried blueberries or cherries (sometimes I use both). A traditional Waldorf salad has grapes and walnuts in it. Below is my version of a Waldorf salad but you can substitute walnuts, dried cranberries, raisins, grapes, mini marshmallows or whatever you want! This is a delicious salad that is versatile and you can whip up in no time. GF

Waldorf Salad

3 apples, I like to use a combo of Honeycrisp and Granny Smith
2 t lemon juice
1 cup diced celery
1 cup chopped pistachios
1 cup dried blueberries or dried cherries
½ cup chopped red onion
¼ cup mayo
¼ cup sour cream or Greek yogurt
½ t salt

Clean and finely dice the apples. Add lemon juice to chopped apples. To the apples, add the next four ingredients. Once combined, fold in the mayo and sour cream/Greek yogurt. Feel free to add more mayo and sour cream/Greek yogurt if you like your salad to be creamier. Add salt and gently mix to combine. Cover and refrigerate for 1 hour or can be made a day ahead.

My sister, Carol, gave me this recipe (with a few tweaks from me). Carol has celiac's disease, so all of her recipes are gluten free. I like to serve this dish with couscous or orzo but they are not gluten free.

Chicken Mediterranean

4 - 6 oz skinless, boneless chicken breasts
2 T olive oil
2 cups grape tomatoes, halved
1 garlic clove, chopped
32 Kalamata olives, halved and seeded
5 T balsamic vinegar
5 T feta cheese, crumbled
4 T fresh basil or 2 t dried
1 t oregano
Salt and pepper to taste

Heat skillet and add olive oil and chicken breasts. Cook breasts 6 minutes per side or until done (165 degrees F). Transfer to serving platter and cover to keep warm. Combine tomatoes, olives, balsamic vinegar, basil and oregano in a bowl. Mix well and add to skillet. Cook 1 to 2 minutes adding garlic last minute of cooking time. Lastly, add feta cheese.

4 Servings

Another recipe from my mom. Sometimes I add tomatoes to it. Great summer salad with burgers, grilled chicken or mediterranean dishes.

Cucumber Salad

3 medium cucumbers peeled and sliced.
1 cup cherry tomatoes, halved, optional
¼ cup vinegar
1 T lemon juice
1 t celery seed
2 T sugar
¾ t salt
⅛ t pepper
¼ to ½ cup chopped onions
2 T chopped fresh parsley or 2 t dried

Mix all ingredients together except cucumbers, add them at the end and gently mix. Marinate and chill for at least two hours stirring occasionally.

6 Servings

I love Shepherd's Pie so much that I have three different versions. GF

Shepherd's Pie 3 Ways

Low Carb Shepherd's Pie

1 lb ground turkey
2 cups carrots, diced
2 cups corn (optional)
1 cup green peas
1 large head cauliflower, chopped into chunks
3 garlic cloves minced
½ cup onion, chopped
¼ cup chives or 1 t dried
1 t oregano
1 t sage
2 T olive oil, divided
Salt and pepper to taste

In a large mixing bowl, toss cauliflower with garlic and 1 T olive oil until cauliflower is well coated. Place cauliflower in pan spreading evenly into a single layer. Roast in a 425 degree oven for 12 minutes. Remove from oven and test cauliflower to make sure it is tender and let cool. Place cooled cauliflower in a food processor and blend to desired consistency. Saute carrots, onions in remaining 1 T olive oil. Add spices and salt and pepper to taste. Once veggies are tender, add corn if using and peas. Set veggies aside and in same pan, brown turkey. Lightly coat a 9 inch pie pan with cooking spray. Spread all the meat in bottom of pan. Add veggies on top of turkey and spread the mashed cauliflower over the top. Bake in 425 degree oven for 20 to 25 minutes until cauliflower begins to brown. Remove from oven and let set for 10 minutes before serving.

4 Servings

Sweet Potato Shepherd's Pie

Same ingredients (minus the cauliflower and ground turkey) as Low Carb Shepherd's Pie
2 sweet potatoes
1 T milk
1 T butter

Follow same directions as cauliflower version but use 2 sweet potatoes instead of cauliflower. Can use your choice of ground turkey or ground beef. Scrub and pierce holes in sweet potato with a fork. Microwave uncovered for 12 minutes, turning once. After cooked, remove skins from sweet potato and mash with fork. Add 1 T milk, 1 T butter. Layer cooked ground beef or turkey in a 9 inch lightly greased pie pan. Add veggies and herbs and spread sweet potato mixture over the top. Bake in a 425 degree oven for 20 – 25 minutes.

4 Servings

Traditional Shepherd's Pie

Same ingredients (minus cauliflower) as Low Carb Sheperd's Pie
3 Idaho or Yukon baking potatoes
1 lb ground beef
2 T (or more if desired) butter
1 T milk

Prepare as cauliflower version of recipe but substitute beef instead of turkey and Idaho/Yukon potatoes instead of cauliflower. Peel potatoes and cut into thirds. Fill a sauce pan with water and bring to a boil. Add potatoes and boil until tender (about 20 minutes). Once tender, remove from pan, drain, mash and add butter, milk and salt and pepper to taste. Place ground beef in a lightly sprayed 9 inch pie pan. Spread cooked veggies over meat. Spread mashed potatoes over the top. Bake in 425 degree oven for 20 -25 minutes.

4 Servings

My mom used to make a similar salad in the winter when I was growing up. It is a nice deviation from a lettuce salad and it pairs perfectly with Shepherd's Pie. GF

Orange Salad With Chives

4 large naval oranges
½ medium onion, diced
1 T apple cider vinegar
1 T extra virgin olive oil
2 t honey
Salt to taste
Pepper to taste
2 T chopped fresh chives for garnish.
Lettuce leaves, optional

Peel oranges and cut each piece in half. Add to a bowl with rest of ingredients except chives. Mix gently and top with chives. Cover and refrigerate until ready to serve. Place on a bed of lettuce, optional but pretty!

4 Servings

I have been making this spaghetti sauce since my kids were toddlers. It is most definitely a kid friendly sauce. A great weeknight meal. Double the recipe and freeze the second batch. Add my tomato, brie and basil salad (recipe on next page) and some garlic bread and you are good to go and everyone in your family will be happy!

Spaghetti Meat Sauce

1 lb ground beef
1 onion, chopped
2 gloves garlic, chopped
28 oz tomato sauce
6 oz tomato paste
¾ cup beef broth or water
2 T fresh basil leaves, chopped or 2 t dried basil
½ cup sugar
8 oz spaghetti noodles
Salt to taste
Shredded parmesan cheese

In a 2 quart saucepan, brown the ground beef with the onion. Add garlic after the meat and onions have been cooking for a few minutes. Drain. Stir in tomato sauce, tomato paste and water or beef broth if using. Add basil and sugar and bring to a boil then simmer for 15 minutes. While sauce is simmering, cook your spaghetti noodles according to package directions. Place noodles on plate, top with sauce and desired amount of parmesan cheese.

Makes 6 servings

A great summer salad and a change of pace from your traditional caprese salad. Super easy to make, delicious and so pretty! GF

Tomato, Brie and Basil Salad

4 cups chopped fresh tomatoes
½ cup yellow cherry tomatoes or red cherry tomatoes
8 oz Brie cheese, rind removed and cut into small cubes
(Not a brie cheese fan? No prob, use diced fresh mozzarella)
1 cup fresh basil leaves chopped or 1 t dried
4 garlic cloves minced
1 T raspberry red wine vinegar or balsamic vinegar
¼ cup olive oil
Salt and pepper to taste

Combine all ingredients in a pretty serving bowl and let sit at room temperature for at least 2 hours so the flavors blend. Can be made several hours ahead of time but just make sure to remove from refrigerator and serve at room temp.

Serves 4 to 6

This is the perfect summer salad for a shower, luncheon or whenever! Colorful, flavorful and wonderful. One of my favorites! The chutney adds the most unique pop of flavor. From the Minneapolis Star Tribune Taste section. If cooking GF, do not use store bought rotisserie chicken.

Chicken Salad With Chutney, Lime and Cilantro

1 (3 lb.) store bought rotisserie chicken or 3 cups cooked chicken breast
½ cup mayonnaise
½ cup mango chutney
¾ cup coarsely chopped walnuts, toasted
½ cup celery, chopped
½ cup red pepper, chopped
½ cup chopped cilantro
3 limes, divided
Pinch of salt
Pinch of pepper
Green leafed lettuce

Remove the skin from the chicken, if using a rotisserie chicken. Cut meat away from bones being careful to remove all the bones. Slice chicken into ¾ inch cubes. Place mayo and chutney (cut any large pieces of mango) in a mixing bowl along with the chicken, walnuts, celery, red bell pepper and cilantro. Juice 2 limes and add 3 T of lime juice to salad and stir to mix. Season with salt and pepper. Cover, refrigerate and chill. Mound chicken on bed of lettuce and garnish with lime wedges or serve on a croissant if not gluten free.

6 Servings

This recipe is a great alternative to beef and tomato based chili. GF

White Chicken Chili

2 onions, finely chopped
1 T olive oil
6 garlic cloves, minced
2 4oz cans diced green chilies
1 T cumin
2 t oregano
½ t cayenne
2 - 15 oz cans northern beans rinsed
6 cups chicken broth
3 to 4 cups shredded chicken
Salt and pepper to taste
1 cup sour cream, for topping
2 cups shredded Monterey Jack cheese, for topping
Additional toppings: green onion, lime wedges, fresh cilantro

Saute onions in olive oil until golden, add garlic. Cook for 1 minute. Drain chilies and add to onion mixture along with cumin, oregano and cayenne. Add beans and broth. Add cooked shredded chicken. Simmer 20 to 30 minutes. Add salt and pepper to taste.

6 Servings

I love me a lettuce salad! This is a great salad dressing that also makes a great marinade for chicken or fish! GF

Honey Balsamic Vinaigrette

½ cup balsamic vinegar
1 small onion finely chopped
1 T coconut aminos
3 T honey
2 cloves minced garlic
1 T fresh basil
½ t crushed red pepper flakes
⅔ cup extra virgin olive oil

Add all ingredients except olive oil to a food processor or blender and mix. Drizzle in olive oil and blend until well combined. Store in airtight container in refrigerator. This dressing can last in refrigerator for up to two weeks.

I love to make this dish on a cold Minnesota winter evening. Serve with rice and my Autumn Apple Salad (recipe on page 44). Thanks for this recipe, Mom!

Chicken Divan

6 chicken breasts sliced in half
2 - 16 oz packages frozen broccoli, well drained
1 ½ cups mayonnaise
⅔ cup half & half
1 ½ cups cheddar cheese, grated
2 cans cream of chicken soup
2 t lemon juice
1 t curry powder
½ cup bread crumbs or cracker crumbs

Place chicken in bottom of a 9x13 baking dish lightly sprayed with cooking spray. Place thawed and drained broccoli over chicken. Mix all other ingredients together (except bread crumbs) and pour over chicken and broccoli. Sprinkle bread crumbs on top. Bake in 350 degree oven for 1 hour.

8 Servings

You can easily make this delicious salad the main entrée by adding grilled chicken. A perfect summertime salad! Fancy enough to serve for a bridal shower! GF

Blueberry and Mango Salad With Greens

⅓ cup dried cherries or cranberries
⅓ cup chopped green onions
⅓ cup chopped pistachios
⅓ cup toasted sliced almonds
8 cups spring greens
1 mango peeled and diced
¾ cup fresh blueberries
4 pounds cooked boneless chicken breast or rotisserie chicken if not gluten free, optional

Dressing:
½ cup vegetable oil or extra virgin olive oil
3 T sugar
½ t salt
½ t pepper
¼ t dried basil
3 T white wine vinegar

Combine the dried fruit, green onions, nuts. Mix together all ingredients for the dressing. Blend well. Place one cup of mixed greens on a plate. Add toppings, sprinkle blueberries and mangos on top and chicken if using. Drizzle dressing over salad.

8 Servings

Thursday

Almost the weekend! More easy entrees and side recipes for you to prepare for your family and gather around the table to eat and talk about your day. Make those memories. You got this!

This is my son, Danny's favorite dish! He always requested it when he would come home from college. It is not your typical enchilada recipe as the recipe calls for whipping cream and cream cheese. I am betting it becomes your favorite recipe too!

Cream Cheese Chicken Enchiladas

2 T butter
2 large onions sliced or chopped
2 cups diced cooked chicken (store bought rotisserie chicken saves time)
½ cup red peppers, chopped
2 cloves garlic, minced
1 t cumin
½ t coriander
8 oz cream cheese, cut into small pieces, room temperature
1 - 4 oz can green chilies, drained
10 to 12 flour tortillas
⅔ cup whipping cream
2 cups shredded Monterey Jack cheese
Lime wedges
Salt and pepper to taste
Garnishes: chopped tomatoes, chopped avocadoes, cilantro, salsa

Preheat oven to 375 degrees. Butter a 9x13 baking pan. In a skillet, melt the butter and sauté onions for 20 minutes adding the chopped red peppers, green chilis and spices the last 10 minutes of cooking time. Add garlic and saute one more minute. Remove from heat and add the cooked chicken. and cream cheese. Mix slightly and season to taste. Spoon about ⅓ cup of chicken filling in center of each tortilla. Roll up and place seam side down in prepared baking pan. Pour cream over enchiladas. Cover tightly with foil and bake 20 minutes. Remove foil and sprinkle with cheese. Bake an additional few minutes until cheese is melted. Squeeze limes on to individual servings. Pairs great with Summer Corn and Black Bean Salad on next page!

6 Servings

This salad is so easy to make and is so colorful. It's my go to salad that I serve with my cream cheese and chicken enchiladas (recipe on previous page). Sometimes I serve it as a salsa with corn chips or with grilled chicken. GF

Summer Corn and Black Bean Salad

1 cup frozen corn (I use Trader Joe's fire roasted frozen corn)
1 - 14 oz can black beans rinsed and drained
½ cup red onion, diced
½ cup red or orange peppers, chopped
½ cup cilantro, chopped (or parsley if you have a cilantro aversion)
½ t cumin
½ t chili powder
1 clove garlic, minced or ¼ t garlic powder
⅛ t cayenne (or more if you like a lot of heat or omit if you don't like heat)
3 T lime juice
2 T olive oil
1 avocado, optional
½ cup chopped cherry tomatoes, optional
Salt to taste

In a small bowl, mix olive oil, lime juice and spices together and set aside. In another larger bowl, add rest of ingredients and pour olive oil and lemon juice mixture over all. Mix until dressing is well combined. Refrigerate for at least an hour to enhance the flavors.

6 Servings

When I was visiting my two sisters in Utah for a ski weekend, my sister, Beth made this chili for dinner after a full day of skiing. It hit the spot and has been my go-to chili recipe ever since! GF

Aunt Beth's Chili

2 lbs ground beef
2 lbs ground mild Italian sausage
2 yellow onions, diced
2 t minced garlic
3 T chili powder
1 t oregano
3 T paprika
1 ½ t cumin
1 t salt
28 oz canned crushed tomatoes
3 cans diced Rotel mild tomatoes
1 small can tomato paste
1 small can diced jalapenos
Toppings: sour cream, cheddar cheese, green onions

Brown meat, onions and garlic in 2 T olive oil. Add spices and rest of ingredients. Bring to a boil and then simmer for 20 minutes, stirring every five minutes. This chili pairs well with my red cabbage and fruit salad on next page!

10 Servings

This salad is so unique and flavorful. The other half of the red cabbage can be used with roasted veggies. Cut into chunks and add to other veggies with olive oil and sea salt and roast in oven at 425 degrees for 20 minutes. Delish! Cabbage lasts a super long time in your refrigerator AND it's a superfood. GF

Red Cabbage and Fruit Salad

½ medium red cabbage
½ cup diced white onion
2 T white wine vinegar or apple cider vinegar
1 ½ t kosher salt
½ mango peeled and diced
1 T maple syrup or honey
2 t olive oil or vegetable oil
1 cup fresh blueberries
½ to ¾ cup fresh raspberries
Optional: fresh mint leaves, chopped

Cut full cabbage in half and save one half for later use. Take remaining half of cabbage and slice in half. Be sure to remove the core and discard. Chop cabbage into thin slices. You will need about 3 cups. You may need to use the other half to equal 3 cups depending on how big the head of cabbage is.

Combine cabbage, onion, vinegar and salt. Stir well. Set aside at room temp to marinate for at least 30 minutes, stirring every five minutes. At end of marinating, fill bowl that cabbage mixture is in with tap water and swirl cabbage to rinse off salt and vinegar. This will lesson the acidity of the vinegar in the salad. Drain then rinse again and drain for 5 minutes. With another bowl, add fruit, maple syrup, oil and drained cabbage mixture (and chopped mint if using). Mix very gently. Chill before serving.

4 Servings

My sister-in-law, Sue gave me this recipe. This is a great dish to serve for Cinco de Mayo parties! Sometimes I will substitute chicken for the beef. You could also make this a vegetarian dish and substitute sautéed vegetables for the meat. I like to double or triple the seasoning portion of this recipe and store extra in a glass container in my pantry. Great on grilled chicken! GF

Mexican Lasagna

1 T chili powder
1 t cumin
½ t coriander
½ t oregano
¼ t paprika
½ t salt
¼ t black pepper
¼ t cayenne
2 T oil

1 onion, chopped
2 cloves garlic, chopped
1 lb lean ground beef
1 cup tomato sauce
3 T canned diced green chiles
4 to 6 cups shredded cheddar cheese
12 - 6 inch corn tortillas
1 can refried or black beans

Preheat oven to 350 degrees. Mix all seasonings together (first 8 ingredients) and set aside. Put oil in a large skillet and cook onions over medium heat until tender. Add garlic and cook another minute. Set onion and garlic aside and to the skillet, add ground beef. Cook until brown and add seasonings, onion and garlic to pan. Mix until combined and then add tomato sauce and chilis. Simmer uncovered for 10 minutes, stirring occasionally.

Spray a 9x13 inch pan with cooking spray and then layer six corn tortillas in bottom of pan. They will overlap. Spread ½ can of refried or black beans (be sure to drain and rinse the black beans) over the tortillas. Spread half of meat (or veggie mixture for vegetarian option), over the beans. Add half of the cheese and repeat layers. Cover with foil. Bake in oven for 25 minutes, remove foil and bake uncovered another 25 minutes or until cheese is bubbly. Let stand 5 to 10 minutes. Top with lettuce, onions, sour cream, avocadoes, peppers, cheese, salsa. Delicious with my mango salsa recipe on next page!

12 Servings

This salsa is wonderful with chips as an appetizer or with grilled fish (mahi mahi) or grilled chicken. I have a batch of this salsa on hand almost all summer long! Can substitute peaches too, especially when the Colorado peaches are in season in August. GF

Mango Salsa

1 to 2 mangoes peeled and cubed
1 avocado cubed
¼ cup red onion chopped
¼ cup cilantro
Juice of one lime
Juice of one orange

Mix ingredients and chill until ready to serve.

4 Servings

My mom gave me this recipe when I called her looking for a pasta recipe that would transport easily as was needing to make it for my daughter's high school hockey team's carbo loads before game day and my son's football team's carbo load. This spaghetti bake was the perfect answer as a little different than lasagna, can be made a day ahead of time and it was /is always a crowd pleaser! No complicated ingredients or directions. It's just a little time consuming to assemble vs my other recipes. Worth the effort!

Spaghetti Bake

2 cups canned diced tomatoes
2 cups tomato sauce
1 cup water
½ cup diced onions
½ cup diced pepper (green red, yellow, or orange)
2 cloves garlic, chopped
¼ cup fresh chopped parsley
2 t Italian seasoning
1 ½ t garlic powder
1 ½ tseasoned salt
1 ½ t sugar
2 small bay leaves
1 ½ lbs ground beef
8 oz uncooked angel hair pasta
1 cup grated cheddar cheese
1 cup grated Monterey jack cheese

In pot, combine tomato sauce, tomatoes, water, onions, peppers and spices. Bring to a boil, then reduce and simmer covered for one hour. Crumble beef in another pan and cook. Drain fat. Add beef to sauce. Simmer for 20 more minutes. Cook pasta according to package directions. Cover bottom of 9x13 pan with sauce. Add a layer of pasta then half of the cheese. Repeat the layers ending with the sauce. Bake at 350 degrees for 30 minutes. Top with remaining cheese, return to oven. Cook until cheese is melted. Let cool for 10 minutes to set then cut into squares. Pairs well with parmesan salad on page 51.

12 Servings

My friend, Amy F. gave me this recipe years ago. I love how easy it is to make but does not skimp on flavor! A great weeknight or weekend meal if cooking for a crowd. It is easy to double this recipe.

Crockpot Chicken Fajitas

1 red pepper, chopped
1 yellow pepper, chopped
1 orange pepper, chopped
1 large onion, chopped
2 cloves garlic, chopped
1 jalapeno pepper, seeds removed, chopped (optional)
1 packet taco or fajita seasoning or my taco seasoning recipe on page 24 of this cookbook
1 lb boneless chicken breasts
½ cup chicken broth
Corn or flour tortillas
Toppings: 8 oz sour cream, 2 avocados, 2 tomatoes, lettuce, 1 jar salsa, 2 cups cheddar cheese, 1 bunch chopped cilantro

Add chopped peppers, onion and garlic to bottom of crockpot. Sprinkle taco or fajita packet over mixture in crockpot. Add the raw chicken. Pour broth over all. Cook on low for 6 to 8 hours. Remove chicken and shred with a fork. Place shredded chicken back into crockpot and mix with veggies.

Serve with warmed corn or flour tortillas and the toppings.

4 Servings

Friday, Saturday, Sunday

Hooray! You made it to the weekend! Wonderful brunch, entrée and side recipes can be found here for entertaining family and friends.

Weekends can be relaxing or chaotic depending on where you are in your life. Whether you are having friends over to watch a football game, or hosting a brunch/dinner party/bridal/baby shower/birthday party, or you are invited to a friend's cabin for the weekend, these Weekend Wonder recipes have you covered. They are all big crowd pleasers and like all of the recipes in this cookbook, not overly complicated or intimidating.

To kick off the Weekend Wonders portion of this cookbook, we are starting with my fabulous brunch recipes. Check them out and give them a go. They are my family favorites and they will quickly become your family favorites too!

This banana bread was inspired from a similar recipe in the Minneapolis Star Tribune. The sour cream is the secret to this delicious recipe and of course, the chocolate chips! Freezes for up to three months!

Banana Bread

1 ½ cups flour
1 t baking soda
1 t salt
1 ½ cups ripe bananas, mashed (about 3 or 4)
½ cup sour cream
1 T vanilla extract
½ cup butter, softened plus extra to grease pan
½ cup granulated sugar
½ cup firmly packed brown sugar
2 eggs
1 cup semi-sweet chocolate chips

Preheat oven to 350 degrees. Grease a standard loaf pan and line bottom with parchment paper (grease first then line with parchment paper.). Lining and greasing the pan will assure the bread doesn't stick to the bottom and sides of the pan. Mix together flour, baking soda and salt. With an electric mixer, beat butter until creamy. Add both kinds of sugar and beat until fluffy. Add eggs and then slowly add flour mixture. Beat on low until flour mixture is combined with rest of the ingredients. Lastly, fold in chocolate chips until well combined. Pour batter into prepared pan and bake for one hour or until top is brown and a toothpick or wooden skewer inserted into the center comes out clean. Set on wire rack to cool for 20 minutes. Using a dull knife, slide knife along edges of pan to loosen the loaf and then invert onto wire rack and flip back over with a plate and finish cooling.

12 Servings

These muffins are perfect for a spring/summer brunch whether entertaining or just for your own family. Another winner from my dear sweet mom!

Lemon Muffins

1 ¾ cup all purpose flour
¾ cup sugar
1 t baking powder
¾ t baking soda
¼ t salt
1 T grated lemon peel
8 oz lemon yogurt (any brand)
6 T butter, melted and cooled
1 large egg, room temperature
1 T lemon juice

Glaze:
⅓ cup lemon juice
¼ cup sugar
2 t grated lemon peel

Preheat oven to 400 degrees. Grease 12x3 inch (regular size) muffin tin cups or use paper liners. In large bowl, combine first six ingredient and in another large bowl, combine the yogurt, melted and cooled butter, egg and lemon juice. Pour wet ingredients into the dry ingredients until just blended. Do not over mix. Batter will be lumpy. Spoon into muffin tins to ¾ way full. Bake for 20 minutes or until muffins are golden brown and toothpick inserted in center of muffin comes out clean (test with muffin in middle of pan). Cool 5 minutes in pan.

For the glaze, cook ingredients in small sauce pan over low heat until sugar dissolves. Remove cooled muffins from pan and place on a rack set over a large baking sheet. Pierce 6 to 8 holes in top of each muffin using a skewer. Drizzle hot glaze over muffins coating them well (the baking sheet will catch all the leftover glaze that spills off of muffin). Serve at room temp.

Makes 12 Muffins

Ever since I was a little kid, my mom baked pumpkin bread at Christmas time for neighbors, friends and of course our family. It was a tradition that I now carry on with my own family and friends. Each recipe makes three loaves of pumpkin bread. The bread freezes wonderfully so can be made ahead of time and kept in freezer for up to three months. Make this your family tradition too!

Pumpkin Bread

3 ⅓ cups flour
2 t baking soda
1 ½ t salt
1 ½ t nutmeg
3 t cinnamon
½ t ginger
1 cup salad oil
4 eggs
⅔ cup water
2 cups canned pumpkin (NOT pumpkin pie filling)
3 cups sugar
2 cups chocolate chops (optional)

Mix all ingredients (except chocolate chips) together preferably with an electric mixer just until blended. Do not over mix. Can be mixed by hand. Gently add chocolate chips if using. Pour into three greased and floured loaf pans (I line the bottom of my loaf pan with parchment paper after I grease it to assure bread doesn't stick to pan). Bake at 350 degrees for 1 hour. Let cool in loaf pan on wire rack. Once cooled, loosen sides with a table knife and ease out carefully onto a flat surface. Once fully cooled, wrap in plastic wrap and if freezing, wrap foil tightly over plastic wrap to prevent freezer burn.

12 Servings per loaf

I am obsessed with scones! They are so very delicious with a cup of coffee in the morning. I prefer them over muffins or donuts. I have toyed and tweaked so many different scone recipes and this one is a keeper. These scones freeze really well. You can make a big batch, keep a few for yourself and freeze the rest for when you have overnight guests or are invited to a friend's cabin for the weekend. Can substitute blueberries or dried cranberries but raspberries for the win.

White Chocolate Raspberry Scones

2 cups flour
2 ½ t baking powder
½ t salt
½ t cinnamon
¼ cup sugar
6 T butter, chilled
1 cup fresh raspberries, rinsed and dried
½ cup white chocolate chips
1 egg slightly beaten combined with enough buttermilk to equal 1 cup

Preheat oven to 400 degrees. Combine flour, baking powder, salt and sugar. Cut cold butter into small chunks and add to mixture and mix until you have course crumbs. Stir in raspberries and white chocolate chips. Stir in egg and buttermilk mixture only until holds together. Add more buttermilk if necessary if too dry and crumbly. Drop by spoonful on to a cookie sheet lined with parchment paper. Bake 10 – 12 minutes. Once done baking, remove scones from cookie sheet and let dry on a rack.

Makes 12 scones

Weekend Wonders/ Brunch

My mom's pancakes are the best! Don't waste your time on store boxed pancake batter. This recipe is easy and so tasty.

Grandma Chapman's Pancakes

2 cups flour
2 T sugar
2 t baking powder
1 t baking soda
½ t salt
2 eggs
2 cups buttermilk
½ cup butter melted
Maple syrup for serving

In a bowl, add dry ingredients together and mix to combine. In a separate bowl, add 2 eggs and slightly beaten. Add 2 cups buttermilk and the melted butter. Add these liquid ingredients to the bowl with the dry ingredients. Stir just to blend. Batter will be slightly lumpy. Let batter rest for at least 15 minutes before cooking. Resting batter allows the flour to absorb the liquid making for lighter and fluffier pancakes. Heat frying pan to 375 degrees. Using a ladle, drop ¼ cup batter on griddle being sure to space batter pours far enough apart as batter will spread. Use back of spoon to spread batter to smooth it into a circle shape. Check underside of pancake after a minute or so. Once golden brown on bottom, flip pancakes with spatula and let other side cook until golden brown. Watch pancakes carefully while cooking as can burn easily. Serve with warmed maple syrup. If you want to make chocolate chip or blueberry pancakes, add these ingredients once you have poured batter onto griddle. Just sprinkle desired amount of whatever ingredient you choose. Other options, chopped walnuts and bananas!

6 Servings

I make this every year on Christmas and Easter morning along with my egg bake. Both dishes are great not only because they are so delicious but also because you can make them a day ahead of time. In the morning, you pop them in the oven, slice up some fruit and you are good to go. My sister-in-law, Laura gave me this recipe years ago, when my kids were little.

Night Before French Toast

1 lb French bread (about 18 inches long)
8 eggs
3 cups whole milk
¼ cup sugar
3 t salt
1 T vanilla
2 T butter cut up into 5 pads
½ t cinnamon (I use a little more)
Maple syrup for serving

Grease a 9x13 inch pan. Cut bread into 18 one inch slices. Arrange slices in bottom of 9x13 pan. Beat eggs, milk, sugar salt and vanilla in large bowl. Pour over bread (bread will be floating on top). Cut each pad of butter into four pieces. Dot each slice of bread with four or so butter pieces. Sprinkle cinnamon over top. Cover and refrigerate overnight. Place dish uncovered in a cold oven. Bake at 350 degrees for 50 minutes. Serve with warm maple syrup.

12 Servings

My mom made egg bakes for every Christmas and Easter morning brunch and now I do the same! The best thing about an egg bake besides how delicious they are, is that you make them a day ahead of time. This is my egg bake recipe using Italian turkey sausage but Italian pork sausage works well too. Either meat adds a robust and savory flavor to this egg bake. You can easily make this a vegetarian egg bake. Broccoli, more red peppers, mushrooms, spinach are my favs. GF

Egg Bake With Italian Turkey Sausage

2 lbs Italian turkey sausage
2 T olive oil
1 cup onion, chopped
1 red pepper diced
8 eggs
4 cups frozen shredded hashbrown potatoes
2 cups whole milk
1 - 4 oz can diced green chilis
2 cups cheddar cheese, shredded, divided
½ t salt
1 t oregano
½ t garlic powder
1 t paprika
1 jar salsa to serve with egg bake

Grease a 9x13 pan. Sweat veggies with 2 T olive oil. Set aside. In same pan as you used for sweating the vegetables, brown the turkey sausage. Set aside. In a large mixing bowl, crack the eggs and mix so whites and yolks are combined. To the eggs in the bowl, add the shredded hashbrown, turkey sausage, one cup of the cheddar cheese, spices, veggies, whole milk and green chilis.. Mix gently to combine. Pour into the greased glass baking dish. Sprinkle remaining one cup of cheese over egg bake. Cover and refrigerate overnight. Can be made 24 hours ahead. Preheat oven to 375 degrees. Place egg bake uncovered in oven and bake for one hour or until top of egg bake is bubbly and browning. Remove from oven and let sit for 10 minutes before cutting. Serve with your favorite salsa.

8 Servings

Bring On the Apps

I can make this with my eyes closed. That is how long and often I have been making this app. Double the recipe as it goes fast!

Artichoke Dip

1 cup shredded parmesan cheese
1 cup mayonnaise
1 cup shredded mozzarella cheese
1 can artichoke hearts cut into small pieces

Mix all ingredients together and place in a glass baking dish. Bake in 350 degree oven for 25 – 30 minutes. Serve with crackers or pita chips.

6 Servings

My friend, Mary H. brought this to my house for a get together several years ago. It's a super easy app to make and the combination of flavors can't be beat. It is one of my kids' favorite apps. If I am serving a big crowd, I double the recipe and put in a 9 x 13 inch pan. Great to serve on football game day!

Buffalo Chicken Dip

2 chicken breasts, cooked, and shredded (about 2 to 2 ½ cups)
½ cup chunky blue cheese dressing
½ cup Frank's hot sauce
8 oz cream cheese, softened
½ cup chopped celery
2 cups cheddar cheese

Mix ingredients together (except cheddar cheese) and place in an 8 or 9 inch tart pan or 8 inch rectangular glass baking dish. Sprinkle cheese on top. Serve with crackers. Bake at 350 for 25 – 30 minutes. I like to use the Big Wheat Thin crackers with this recipe. Pita chips work well too.

My college gal pals at one of our monthly potluck gatherings. Photo by LaPanta Photography.

This recipe is from my college friend, Andrea. We started a potluck with my University of St. Thomas college friends. We still gather monthly (35 plus years later) and our group grew from five women to seventeen women! All college friends. I am blessed to have these beautiful strong group of women in my life who gather monthly to break bread.

Boboli With Caramelized Onions

1 thin store bought Boboli crust
1 medium red onion, thiny sliced
4 T butter
½ cup brown sugar
1 t salt
1 t pepper
½ cup chopped pecans
¾ cup gorgonzola cheese

In medium sauce pan, sauté onions and butter until caramelized and golden brown. Add brown sugar, salt, pepper and stir until mixture is gooey. Turn heat to low. Add pecans and stir another minute. Remove from heat and bring mixture to room temperature (this part can be done day before). Spread onion mixture evenly over Boboli crust. Crumble cheese all over pecan mixture. Bake at 400 degrees until slightly bubbles (about 10 minutes). Cool, slice and serve at room temperature.

8 Servings

My college friend and roommate, Colleen served this at a dinner party and I was hooked from the first mouthful. We are talking REALLY, REALLY good. Addicting in fact. Can be made any time of year. Super easy and makes a huge serving. Also, if I had a dollar for how many times my daughter asked me for this recipe. Now you have it in one place, Molly! GF

Everyone's Favorite Corn Dip

3 cans Mexicorn, drained
2 cups mild cheddar cheese
¾ cup sour cream
¾ cup mayonnaise
1 bunch cilantro
1 bunch green onions, tops and all
Cayenne pepper to taste (optional)
Serve with Frito Scoops

Mix all ingredients together and chill for a few hours. Can be made a day ahead of time.

16 Servings

This is my mom's recipe and I have been making it for years. Way better than store bought dill dip. Easy to make and your guests will appreciate your effort in making a homemade dip. I serve it with veggies but bagel chips would be good too! GF

Dill Dip

1 cup sour cream
1 cup mayo
2 t dried dill weed or 4 T fresh, finely chopped
2 T dried minced onion
1 T dried parsley
1 T garlic powder
⅛ t salt

Mix all ingredients together and chill. Serve with cut up veggies.

6 Servings

This salsa recipe comes from my friend and former neighbor, Nancy B. It always gets devoured right away when I serve it. So delicious and a bit different from traditional salsa in that it has a Mediterranean twist. This would also be good served with a grilled chicken breast as an entrée!

Fiesta Salsa

2 plum tomatoes chopped
1 avocado halved and chopped
¼ cup chopped red onion
1 clove garlic, minced
1 T parsley
1 T fresh oregano or 1 t dried
1 T olive oil
1 T red or white wine vinegar
4 oz feta crumbled feta cheese

In medium bowl, combine tomatoes, avocado, onion, garlic, spices oil and vinegar. Stir gently to mix. Stir in feta cheese. Cover and chill for 2 hours. Serve with tortilla or pita chips.

6 Servings

This is my mom's recipe and she gave to me when I called her in a panic, as I needed to bring an app for my first ever college potluck in 1990! It's simple and delicious with only three ingredients and stands the test of time!

Hot Brie Cheese With Chutney

4 inch round of brie cheese
½ cup Major Grey's Chutney
½ lb cooked bacon, chopped

Place brie cheese in casserole dish, spread chutney on top being careful not to spread to the edges (no need to cut top off brie cheese). Sprinkle bacon on top. Bake in 350 degree oven for 30 minutes or until bubbly.
Serve with crackers of your choice.

6 Servings

Don't let the length of this recipe intimidate you! You CAN make this appetizer. Yes, it's a little bit fussy in terms of prep, but I promise the lucky peeps that get to eat this appetizer will be forever grateful. No kidding, it's that good!

Layered Asian Dip

Sauce
¼ cup firmly packed brown sugar
2 t cornstarch
1 cup water
¼ cup ketchup
1 T Worcestershire sauce
A few drops of red pepper hot sauce
2 T vinegar

Topping
¾ cup chopped cooked chicken
½ cup finely shredded or chopped carrot
⅓ cup chopped red pepper
¼ cup chopped peanuts, unsalted
3 T chopped green onions
1 T chopped fresh parsley
2 t coconut aminos for gluten free option
¼ t ground ginger or 1 t fresh minced fresh ginger
1 garlic clove, minced
½ cup chopped cilantro, optional

Bottom Layer
8 oz cream cheese, softened
1 T milk

Serve with a sturdy cracker. You will want to load all this goodness on it!

Combine the brown sugar and cornstarch in a small pan. Cook on medium heat and add the water, ketchup, vinegar, Worcestershire sauce and hot sauce. Heat for 5 minutes or until the mixture thickens slightly, stirring frequently. Let stand until cool. Chill, covered until ready to use. Sauce will thicken a bit in the refrigerator.

For the topping, combine all ingredients in a bowl and mix well. Chill covered for a few hours. For the bottom layer, combine the cream cheese and milk in a mixing bowl. Beat until smooth and fluffy. Spread this mixture on the bottom of a 10 inch round serving dish. Spoon the topping evenly over the cream cheese. Drizzle with ½ or more of the sauce, reserving the rest of the sauce for stir fry later in the week or for a dip with air fried chicken tenders!

10 Servings

A super easy appetizer that is great to serve around the holiday season. Short cut would be to purchase premade meatballs but if you make your own, you won't regret it. Compliments galore! Another tried and true recipe from the Dubuque Symphony Orchestra fund raising cookbook that my mom gave me when I was newly married.

Meatballs With Cranberry Sauce

Meatballs:
2 lbs ground beef
1 cup cracker crumbs (I use Ritz)
1 cup chopped fresh parsley or 1/3 cup dried
2 T soy sauce
½ t garlic powder
2 T minced dried onion flakes
2 eggs
⅓ cup ketchup
Pinch of pepper

Combine meatball mixture and form into medium size balls. Place on a parchment lined baking sheet and bake in a 350 degree oven for 30 to 35 minutes.

Sauce:
16 oz jellied cranberry sauce
12 ounces chili sauce
2 T brown sugar
1 T lemon juice
In saucepan, combine sauce ingredients and cook over medium heat stirring occasionally until mixture is dissolved and mixed together.

Place cooked meatballs in crockpot and pour sauce over meatballs. Keep crockpot on warm and serve right away or in a few hours and throughout your gathering/party. Makes a great appetizer because it can be made way ahead of time and will stay warm in the crockpot.

12 Servings

This is a standard app in the Callahan house. It makes a big batch, is easy and everyone loves it! I got the recipe from Ann K, a mom of my son, Charlie's college baseball teammate.

Mustard Pretzel Dip

1 cup mayonnaise
1 cup sour cream
1 cup yellow mustard
½ cup sugar
1 packet Ranch dip seasoning mix
1 packet Lipton onion soup mix

Combine all ingredients and refrigerate. Serve with waffle style pretzels, as it can fit a lot of dip on the surface and the dip also seeps into the open squares! Can be made a day or two ahead of time.

10 Servings

Another staple at the Callahan house. This recipe comes from my sister, Cathy and is a huge crowd pleaser. Double this recipe as it disappears quickly! Waffle style pretzels work the best with this dip or a spoon!

Cream Cheese Pretzel Dip

1 beaten egg
2 T vinegar
3 T sugar
8 oz cream cheese
½ onion chopped
¼ green onion chopped

Cook egg, vinegar and sugar over medium heat until mixture thickens (careful not to overcook the egg as you don't want it to scramble). Remove from heat and let cool. Add onion and pepper to cooled mixture. Serve with pretzels.

6 Servings

This is great as a veggie or chip dip but also delicious on a baked potato or on potato wedges.

Seasoned Sour Cream Dip

1 cup mayo
1 cup sour cream
2 T lemon juice
2 T Worcestershire sauce
½ t dried parsley
½ t garlic salt
½ t paprika
½ t salt
¼ t cayenne pepper
¼ t pepper

Mix all ingredients together and refrigerate for a few hours before serving.

8 Servings

The perfect app for a summer party! It looks and tastes delicious! Double this recipe as it gets devoured quickly! Another winner from my college potluck group. Thank you, Jill O! GF

Shrimp Salsa

1 T butter
2 T olive oil
3 T lime juice
1 T sugar
½ t salt
½ lb raw shrimp cut into bite sized pieces, tails removed
1 T butter
½ cup red pepper chopped
½ cup yellow or orange pepper chopped
¼ cup cilantro chopped
¼ cup scallions chopped
2 T minced garlic
1 avocado chopped

Saute shrimp in butter until shrimp turns pink (no more than five minutes). Stir frequently. Cool. Mix marinade and add cooked and cooled shrimp. Add remaining ingredients except avocado. Marinate for 6 hours or overnight. Add avocado just before serving. Serve with corn tortilla chips.

6 Servings

I like to go strawberry picking in June in Minnesota. One of my favorite things to make with all of my strawberries is strawberry mango salsa. Great served with sturdy chips, chicken or fish. I usually triple this recipe! GF

Strawberry Mango Salsa

¾ cup strawberries
¾ cup mangoes
1 jalapeno, seeded and minced
2 T diced red onion
2 T cilantro
2 t honey
Juice of one lime

Mix ingredients together and chill until ready to serve with corn tortilla chips.

6 Servings

My sister-in-law, Karen always brings this delicious dip to holiday gatherings. My kids are always excited to dive in! GF

Toffee Apple Dip

¾ firmly packed brown sugar
½ cup powdered sugar
1 t vanilla extract
8 ounces cream cheese, softened
¾ cup toffee bits
4 apples cut into wedges (cut apples right before serving)

Beat brown sugar, powdered sugar, vanilla and cream cheese in a mixing bowl until well blended. Stir in toffee bits. Cover and chill in refrigerator. When ready to serve, spoon dip into serving bowl and serve with apple wedges.

6 Servings

The spinach, pepper, chilis and tomatoes add the right amount of panache to this festive holiday appetizer. GF

Zesty Spinach Dip

2 T vegetable oil
1 onion, chopped
2 tomatoes, chopped
¼ cup chopped red pepper, chopped
1 t minced onion
1 - 4 oz can chopped green chilis
1 - 10 oz package frozen spinach, thawed
2 cups shredded Monterey Jack cheese
8 oz cream cheese softened and cut into ½ inch pieces
1 cup half-and-half
2 - 2 oz cans sliced black olives (optional)
1 T red wine vinegar
½ t garlic powder
1 t cumin
Salt to taste
Freshly ground pepper to taste
Tortilla chips or crackers

Heat oil in heavy skillet over medium heat. Add the onion and chopped red pepper and sauté for 4 minutes or until softened,. Add minced garlic, tomatoes and green chilis. Stir and cook or 1 minute. Press the excess moisture from the spinach. Combine the cooked veggies, spinach, and rest of ingredients. Spoon into a tart dish or other shallow ovenproof dish. Bake at 400 degrees for 35 minutes or until bubbly and top is browned. Serve with tortilla chips or crackers.

Can be made up to two days ahead of time and refrigerated before baking.

8 Servings

Weekend Wonder Entrees

I love entertaining on the weekends! Whether my grown kids are coming over for Sunday dinners or we are hosting a dinner party, all of the entrees in this section will keep your family and your friends eager to be invited over again and again!

This is a great summer salad as you can use fresh tomatoes from your garden or the farmer's market! Not only is this salad easy to make and very tasty, it makes a huge batch so great for serving a large crowd. I was inspired by a similar recipe from The Best of Byerly's Cookbook. I made a few changes to the original recipe and this dish has been my go -to salad for years. I have made for my kids' high school graduation parties, large family get togethers, weekends at friends' cabins and bridal/baby showers.

Pasta Salad With Tomatoes & Feta

1 - 16 oz package uncooked penne pasta
1 T salt
1 t oregano
1 - 8 oz bottle Zesty Italian dressing
2 cups tomatoes, chopped
1 - 7 oz jar sun-dried tomatoes in oil, drained, chopped (about ½ cup)
2 - 4 oz packages crumbled feta cheese
½ cup fresh basil, chopped
¼ cup capers
¼ cup parmesan cheese

Cook pasta in boiling salted water until almost tender, about 11 minutes. Drain pasta and rinse with cold water. Drain again. In large bowl, combine the pasta and dressing. Gently stir in remaining ingredients. Refrigerate covered several hours or overnight.

28 ½ Cup servings

I have been making these sandwiches since my kids were in elementary school. Another mom from where my kids went to school, gave me this recipe. Thank you, Mary T! Serve With Penne Pasta Tomatoes and Feta salad (recipe on page103). Can be assembled a day ahead.

Hot Ham & Swiss Sandwiches

1 ½ lbs shaved ham
1 lb swiss cheese
24 dollar buns

Sauce:
2 sticks butter
2 T dry mustard
3 T Worcestershire sauce
½ cup brown sugar

Assemble sandwiches (swiss, ham swiss) and place in greased 9x13 greased baking pan. Mix sauce in saucepan and bring to a boil. Drizzle sauce over sandwiches. Cover with foil and refrigerate for at least 4 hours. Bake covered at 350 degrees for 25 minutes. Remove foil and bake an additional 5 minutes.

12 Servings

I have tried so many barbeque rib recipes just to try to switch things up but I always keep coming back to this recipe of my mom's. It was a family favorite growing up and is my kids' and husband's favorite as well. The meat literally falls off the bone. This recipe originated from Finley Hospital in Dubuque, Iowa where I grew up! My dad was a doctor and was doing rounds over the dinner hour at the hospital. He went to the hospital cafeteria for a quick bite to eat between seeing patients and had these spare ribs. He was so in awe of their deliciousness that he asked the head cook in the kitchen of the hospital for the recipe and luckily for our family, he obliged!

Best BBQ Ribs Ever

3 to 4 lbs baby back spare ribs
2 medium sized onions, sliced
1 T vinegar
1 T salt
2 T Worcestershire sauce
½ t black pepper
1 T chili powder
1 cup chili sauce
½ cup brown sugar
1 t paprika
1 cup ketchup
¾ cup water
½ t liquid smoke (use sparingly)

Trim fat from ribs and cut into serving sizes. Arrange in roaster. Spread onions over the ribs. Mix rest of ingredients together and pour over ribs and onions. Place covered in oven for 2 ½ to 3 hours at 350 degrees. 15 minutes before removing from oven, remove lid from roaster and bake uncovered. Baste frequently while cooking.

4 to 6 Servings

This casserole is a Mexican version of lasagna. You can make it a day ahead and chill in refrigerator. I have made this for family meals and for dinner parties and served with chips, salsa, guacamole and of course margaritas! This pairs really well with my Summer Corn and Black Bean Salad (recipe on page 71).

Enchilada Casserole

2 T olive oil
1 onion, chopped
½ cup red pepper, chopped
2 cloves garlic, minced
2 lbs ground beef or shredded chicken
12 oz can Mexicorn
2 t salt
1 t dried oregano
1 t cumin
½ t dried rosemary
1 t coriander
1 - 16 oz can tomato sauce
2 - 10 oz cans enchilada sauce
12 flour tortillas
3 cups shredded Monterey Jack cheese
Serve with salsa, sour cream and cilantro

Preheat oven to 350. In skillet, cook beef until browned. Drain and set aside. Add oil to skillet and onions and peppers. Saute vegetables until tender. Add garlic and stir one more minute and then add beef back to skillet, seasonings and the corn. Mix well and simmer on low heat for 10 minutes. In a mixing bowl, combine tomato sauce, enchilada sauce and pour half over meat mixture in skillet. Set remaining mixture aside. Simmer another 5 minutes. In bottom of a greased 9x13 pan, arrange 6 tortillas. They will overlap. Pour meat mixture over tortillas and sprinkle half of cheese over meat. Cover with remaining tortillas. Sprinkle remaining cheese and pour remaining sauce over all. Cover with foil and bake for 30 minutes.

If casserole was made day before and refrigerated, bake for 45 minutes.

12 Servings

This is a great recipe from the Byerly's cookbook. I have served this for bridal and baby showers, lunch gatherings and for family meals in the spring and summer months. You can substitute turkey for the chicken if desired. You can also omit the pasta and serve the salad on a croissant. This recipe serves a lot of people.

Chicken Cherry Pasta Salad

2 lbs boneless chicken breasts cooked and cubed
16 oz pasta bow tie pasta
½ red onion sliced or diced
¾ cup celery, thinly sliced
1 - 5oz pkg. dried cherries
1 ¼ cup mayonnaise
1 ¼ cup creamy poppy seed dressing (I use Brianna's)
1 ½ t salt
¼ t pepper
4 cups baby spinach, stems removed
1 cup chopped walnuts, toasted (or almonds slivered or sliced)

Combine chicken, pasta, onion, celery and cherries. In a separate bowl combine mayo, poppy seed dressing, salt and pepper. Fold 1 ¾ cup dressing into salad reserving ¾ cup dressing. Refrigerate covered several hours or overnight.

To serve: fold in spinach and walnuts; add remaining dressing as needed.

Makes 16 ½ cup servings

This beef kabob recipe originated from my mom but I made a few tweaks to it. I remember having these kabobs as a kid in the summertime. My mom would make the marinade and assemble the kabobs. My dad would grill and get all the credit! Funny how that works! I always make the kabobs a day ahead. Letting the kabobs sit in that marinade really enhances the flavor. Serve with a big tossed salad with my homemade salad dressing (recipe on page 66) and either my roasted red potatoes or cheesy potatoes (recipes on pages 116 & 117). Yes, the kabobs are time consuming to make but the perfect summer meal for when you are entertaining. They are so pretty and easy to grill! Your family and friends will appreciate your efforts! GF

Beef Kabobs

For the marinade

½ cup olive oil
½ cup coconut aminos
2 T vinegar
2 T dried minced onion,
2 T fresh ginger, minced or
½ t dried ginger
⅛ t garlic powder

For the kabobs

2 lbs beef sirloin or tenderloin (I like tenderloin as way more tender but more expensive) cut into ¾ inch cubes
1 red pepper
1 yellow pepper
1 red onion
1 pineapple (canned pineapple works too!)
8 oz container mushroom caps
8 kabob skewers (if using wooden skewers, soak in cold water for ½ hour before assembling kabobs as prevents skewers from catching on fire when grilling and prevents splintering of the skewer)

Wash veggies and cut peppers, onion and pineapple into 1 or 2 inch chunks. Assemble kabobs in any order being sure to create a colorful kabob. I usually put the red onion next to beef as great combo when eaten together! Place kabobs in a pan with at least a two inch edge. Pour marinade over kabobs, wrap in foil and marinate for several hours, basting and rotating kabobs at least once. Cook over medium high grill for 8 to 10 minutes, rotating half way through.

8 Servings

Weekend Wonders/ Entrees

Another recipe winner from my mom. Easy to make but tastes like you grinded all day in the kitchen preparing it. Pour extra sauce over mashed potatoes or rice. This recipe pairs nicely with brussel sprouts (recipe on page 119). Yumskles!

Pork Tenderloin With Apricot Preserves

1 - 12 oz jar apricot preserves
2 T dry sherry
1 T dry mustard
2 T honey
½ t garlic powder
2 lbs pork tenderloin
½ cup butter
2 t dry thyme

Combine first five ingredients. Stir well and set aside. Place tenderloins in a pan, spread tenderloins with butter and sprinkle with thyme. Bake at 350 for 40 – 45 minutes. Remove from oven and baste with sauce. Bake additional 15 minutes or until done. Basting every 5 minutes.

6 Servings

This is my mom's recipe and I had it as a kid and continue to make it as an adult. Delicious served with mashed potatoes. Great for Sunday family dinners or for entertaining friends.

Pork Tenderloin in Mushroom Sauce

2 whole pork tenderloins (3 lbs total) floured and seasoned with salt and pepper
½ cup butter softened
1 cup cream of mushroom soup
½ can (using the soup can that mushroom soup was in) sherry
½ lb fresh mushrooms

Dredge tenderloins in flour to coat (but not too thick). Melt butter in skillet and add tenderloins and cook until browned. Remove tenderloins on to a plate. Add mushrooms and sautee. Add mushroom soup and sherry. Place tenderloins in an oven proof dish and pour sauce over tenderloins. Cover and bake at 350 for one hour. Baste tenderloins with sauce every 20 minutes.

6 Servings

When I visit my sisters, Carol and Beth in Utah in the winter, we always ski at Deer Valley ski resort. When taking a lunch break, I look forward to Deer Valley's famous turkey chili. It is so hearty and flavorful. I found this copycat recipe online and made a few changes to it. GF

Close To Deer Valley Turkey Chili

½ cup unsalted butter
2 medium Anaheim chili peppers, seeded and chopped
1 cup red onion, chopped
1 cup celery, chopped
1 cup red bell pepper, chopped
1 large leek, white part only, chopped (optional)
2 cloves garlic, minced
2 t dried oregano
¼ cup corn flour
1 t cayenne pepper
2 ½ T ground cumin
2 T ground coriander
1 t salt
1 t pepper
⅛ cup sugar
4 ½ cups chicken stock, divided
2 ¼ cups frozen corn, thawed, divided
4 cups cooked turkey or chicken, diced
2 - 15 oz cans black beans, rinsed and drained
Toppings: shredded cheddar cheese, green onions, sour cream, cilantro

Sweat veggies in butter in stock pot. Add garlic to vegetables at end of cooking time. Mix corn flour into veggie mixture. Add spices, turkey and 4 cups of chicken stock. Bring to a boil, simmer for 5 minutes. Puree 1 ¼ cup of the corn with ¼ cup chicken stock. Add 1 cup of corn, and the pureed corn to the chili. Simmer for 25 minutes. Add black beans at end of cooking time.

8 Servings

Weekend Wonders/
Entrees

My husband, Charlie loves beef stew and he is always craving it in the colder months in Minnesota. This is my version of beef stew. Serve with naan bread for dipping! Quintessential comfort food for Sunday dinners. I love to serve it with my Waldorf Salad (recipe on page 57).

Crockpot Beef Stew

2 lbs stew meat or steak cut in to 1 inch cubes (I buy good quality beef as more tender)
1 large sweet potato, peeled and cut into chunks
2 carrots, peeled and diced
1 parsnip, peeled and diced
1 large onion, chopped
1 red pepper chopped
1 cup frozen peas
4 garlic cloves, minced
½ t thyme
1 t paprika
1 bay leaf
2 T balsamic vinegar
1 cup red wine
1 ½ cups beef broth
1 T tomato paste
1 package Lipton Onion Soup Mix
2 T cornstarch
Salt and pepper to taste

Place all ingredients in crock pot, except cornstarch. Mix well. Cover and cook on low for 8 to 10 hours or on high 4 to 6 hours. Stir occasionally. When meat is cooked and veggies are tender, turn stew down to warm and make your cornstarch slurry (cornstarch mixed with some of the beef broth stew,) add slurry back to stew and stir well. This will thicken the stew after about 15 minutes or so on warm. Remove bay leaf before serving.

Serves 6

The Side Show

With the Weekend Wonder Entrees, it is really important to add a side. It balances out the meal and makes your dinner more aesthetically pleasing, which is what you want to do when entertaining.

All of the potato recipes in this chapter pair well with any Weekend Wonder meat entrée. Throw in a lettuce salad (because you need something green on your plate) and you are now ready to wow your family members and friends this weekend! Way to go and yay you!

This is an easy dish to serve to a large crowd. Can be made a day ahead and reheated. Everyone loves this and it pairs great with any meat dish.

Roasted Red Potatoes

5 lbs red potatoes quartered
¼ cup olive oil
1 package Lipton Onion Soup Mix
1 package Hidden Valley Ranch Seasoning Salad Dressing Mix
¾ cup fresh parmesan cheese (optional)
3 T parsley

Preheat oven to 400 degrees. Toss potatoes in olive oil first then when well coated, add in the packets of seasoning. Toss well to coat. Place in a roaster and roast for one hour, stirring potatoes every fifteen minutes. Top with parmesan cheese and parsley at end of cooking time.

10 Servings

My mom made these all the time when I was growing up. Every time my dad grilled burgers, my mom made these baked beans. It was her mom's recipe so has been around a very long time and still a family favorite!

Grandma's Baked Beans

1 - 32 oz can baked beans (I use Van Camp's)
3 slices uncooked bacon cut into small pieces
¾ cup brown sugar
1 to 2 T molasses
2 drops liquid smoke
2 slices onions chopped
2 T ketchup
Dash of Worcestershire sauce

Mix all ingredients together and place in baking dish for 2 hours at 325 degrees, stirring occasionally. Reduce oven to 250 degrees and bake one more hour.

6 Servings

This cheesy potato dish pairs really well with kabobs, grilled chicken, or bbq ribs. GF

Cheesy Red Potatoes With A Kick

1 ½ lbs small red potatoes
1 T olive oil
¼ cup butter
1 T flour
1 cup milk
1 - 8 oz Mexican style Veleveeta cheese, cubed
2 garlic cloves, minced
½ cup red pepper, chopped
½ cup onion, chopped
¼ t salt
¼ t pepper
¼ t red pepper flakes (optional)
1 ½ t dried parsley

Preheat oven to 350 degrees. Cook potatoes in boiling water covered for 20 minutes. Let cool and then cut into thin slices. Set aside. In same pan, add olive oil, onions and peppers. Sautee until tender, adding the minced garlic at very end cooking for one minute. Remove from pan and set aside. In same pan, melt butter over low heat, whisking in flour until smooth. Gradually whisk in milk, salt, pepper and red pepper flakes. Cook over medium heat until slightly thickened and bubbly. Remove from heat. Add cubed cheese and mix until melted. Layer in an 8 inch greased square dish or oval dish, potatoes and veggie mixture. Pour melted cheese mixture over the top. Sprinkle with parsley. Place in oven for 30 minutes.

Serves 6

There are so many cheesy potato recipes out there but this is my family's favorite. The Frosted Flakes on the top are unexpected but so good. Thank you, Mary F. for this recipe!

Cheesy Hash Brown Potatoes

2 lb bag of frozen shredded hash browns
2 cans cream of potato or cream of chicken soup
1 - 8 oz carton sour cream
16 oz shredded cheddar cheese
1 small onion chopped
Salt and pepper to taste
2 cups crushed Frosted Flakes for topping (yes, Frosted Flakes, they're GRRREAT!)

Grease a 9x13 pan. Spread the frozen hash browns on bottom of pan. Sprinkle a hand full of cheese over potatoes. In a separate bowl, combine soup, sour cream, onion and another handful of cheese. Spread this over the cheese covered hash browns. Sprinkle remaining cheese on top. Bake in 350 degree oven for about 45 minutes. Sprinkle the crushed Frosted Flakes over the top and bake another 10 minutes.

12 Servings

Anyone who knows me knows I am obsessed with brussels sprouts! If we are out to dinner, my family and friends laugh as I am always suggesting brussels sprouts for an app or a side dish. This is a super easy brussels sprout recipe from Ina Garten (Food Network). This side dish is easy to pair with any entrée. I make it all the time and everyone loves it! Sometimes I will sprinkle the brussels sprouts with shredded parmesan cheese or a balsamic glaze with a sprinkle of pistachios for an added crunch! GF

Brussels Sprouts

1 ½ lbs brussels sprouts
3 T olive oil
¾ t salt
½ t black pepper

Rinse, dry and cut brussels sprouts into halves or thirds depending on size. Add rest of ingredients to cut brussels sprouts and spread in a thin layer on a large cookie sheet covered with parchment paper. Roast in 400 degree oven for 35 to 40 minutes mixing half way through roasting time.

6 Servings

Easy and Delicious. Mic drop. GF

Roasted Asparagus With Parmesan Cheese and Lemon

2½ lbs fresh asparagus
2 T olive oil
½ t kosher salt
¼ t black pepper
½ cup freshly grated parmesan cheese
2 lemons cut in wedges

Cut off any stalks for asparagus that are too thick. Lay in a single layer on a sheet pan over parchment paper. Drizzle with olive oil. Sprinkle with salt and pepper. Roast for 15 to 20 minutes or until tender, careful not to overcook. You don't want mushy asparagus! Remove from oven and sprinkle with parmesan cheese. Squeeze lemon juice over asparagus and serve immediately.

8 Servings

Twice baked potatoes are a little laborious but such a treat to make for a holiday or for company. There are a lot of twice baked potato recipes out there but this one is my mom's and I think it's the best! GF

Twice Baked Potatoes

4 large baking potatoes
¾ cup sour cream
6 T butter, melted
2 oz cream cheese, softened
2 green onions
1 t salt
1 t pepper
¼ t thyme
¼ cup whole milk
¾ cup grated cheddar cheese
Dash of paprika

Scrub and pierce potatoes and bake them whole for 1 hour in 400 degree oven. Remove from oven and cool. Until cooled off enough to handle, cut in half and carefully scoop out potato filling. Place in a bowl and place shells of potatoes on a cookie sheet or shallow casserole dish. To the potato filling, add rest of ingredients mixing well to combine. Gently fill each potato shell with the potato mixture. Top each potato with a light sprinkle of paprika. Bake in a 350 degree oven for 20 minutes

8 Servings

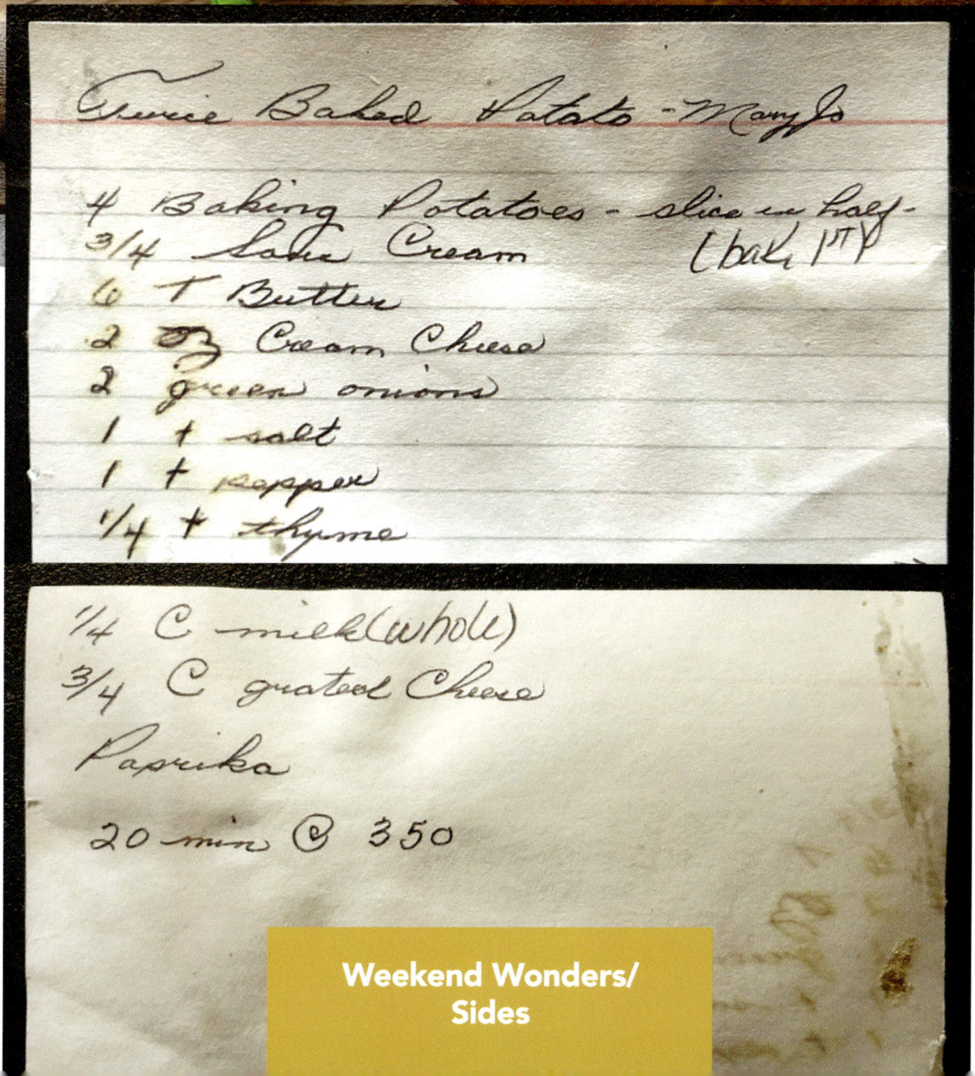

Twice Baked Potato - Mary Jo

4 Baking Potatoes - slice in half (bake 1st)
3/4 Sour Cream
6 T Butter
2 oz Cream Cheese
2 green onions
1 t salt
1 t pepper
1/4 t thyme

1/4 C milk (whole)
3/4 C grated Cheese
Paprika

20 min @ 350

Sweets For Your Sweets! Any Day Of The Week!

I have baked so many desserts over the years for my family and friends. The desserts I chose for this cookbook are my tried and true sweets that everyone devours whenever I make them! Give them a go any day of the week!

These bars are so good, easy to make and freeze well. Double the batch and freeze second batch for another time. When freezing, be sure to store in an airtight container and layer with parchment paper so bars do not stick together. Also, be sure bars are fully cooled before placing in freezer to prevent freezer burn. Can be stored in freezer for up to three months!

M.K.'s Butterscotch Marshmallow Bars

1 package yellow cake mix
⅓ cup oil
2 eggs
1 - 12oz bag butterscotch chips
2 cups white chocolate chips
1 bag mini marshmallows
½ cup butter
1 - 14 oz can sweetened condensed milk

Heat oven to 350 degrees. Grease a 9x13 inch pan. In a large bowl, combine the cake mix, oil and eggs and mix well. Stir in in butterscotch chips and white chocolate chips. Spread half of the mixture into a 9x13 inch well greased pan. Bake for 10 minutes.

While half of the bars are baking, time to make your filling. In a medium saucepan, combine the butter, marshmallows and sweetened condensed milk. Cook over medium low heat until marshmallows are melted. Stir until smooth. Remove partial bars from oven and pour marshmallow mixture over the crust. Crumble remaining mix over the marshmallow mixture.

Place in oven and bake for 25 minutes or until top is set and edges are pulling away from pan and are golden brown. Cool for 15 minutes and run knife along sides to loosen bars from pan. Cool another 30 plus minutes and cut into bars.

12 Servings

These brownies are my go-to for any time. I have been making these since my kids were toddlers. Great served with vanilla ice cream. Another winner from my mom! I like to double this recipe and freeze the other batch for another time. Can be frozen for up to three months. Cut into servings and layer in a plastic container with parchment paper.

Caramel Brownies

1 package German chocolate cake mix
1 stick butter melted
⅔ cup evaporated milk, divided
¾ cup chocolate chips
50 light caramels or 2 ⅛ cups caramel bits.

In a bowl, mix together chocolate cake mix with butter and ⅓ cup evaporated milk. Pat ½ of this mixture into a well greased and floured 9x13 inch pan (or grease pan and put parchment paper on bottom of pan to help keep brownies from sticking). Bake 6 minutes at 350 degrees. Melt caramels and remaining ⅓ cup of evaporated milk in small pan on stove. Keep on low heat stirring frequently to prevent mixture from burning. Sprinkle chocolate chips onto crust when removed from oven. Over chips, pour melted caramel mixture. Over caramel mixture, crumble remaining brownie dough over top. Bake 18 to 20 minutes at 350 degrees. Cool completely before cutting into squares.

12 Servings

My mom always made this frozen cheesecake for dessert on Christmas Day since I was a kid. Always a hit with family and friends, even non cheesecake lovers! I make it year round!

Frozen No Bake Cheesecake

2 cups graham cracker crumbs, divided
2 - 8 oz cream cheese, room temp
2 cups and 2 T sugar, divided
6 egg yolks
6 egg whites
2 t vanilla extract
Pinch of salt
2 cups whipping cream
12 oz frozen raspberries

In a 9x13 inch pan, sprinkle half of the graham cracker crumbs. Mix cream cheese, sugar, yolks vanilla and salt. Gently mix in softened cream cheese. In a separate bowl, whip the egg whites until stiff peaks form. Gently fold whipped egg whites into the cream cheese mixture. Next, whip the whipping cream until soft peaks form. Gently fold this into the cream cheese mixture. Once well combined, pour into pan and sprinkle the remaining graham cracker crumbs over the top. Place in freezer for at least two hours or up to a month. When ready to serve, remove from freezer and let cheesecake thaw for fifteen minutes as easier to cut (no longer as cheesecake will be too soft and lose its shape). Place thawed raspberries in a bowl with the remaining two tablespoons of sugar and mix. Place a generous spoonful of raspberries over each individually sliced piece of cheesecake. Serve and hear the oohs and ahhs!

Note: Recipe uses raw eggs.

12 Servings

Another great recipe from the Minneapolis Star Tribune! I love making this pound cake in the summer as the lemon flavor pairs perfectly with summertime vibes!

Pound Cake

2 cups flour
¼ t baking powder
¼ t salt
1 ⅛ cups sugar, divided
1 cup (2 sticks) butter, softened
4 eggs, well beaten
Grated rind of 1 lemon
2 t vanilla
3 cups fresh or frozen strawberries or raspberries for garnish
Whipped cream for topping

If using fresh strawberries or raspberries, rinse strawberries or raspberries. Gently pat dry with a paper towel. Place fruit in bowl and sprinkle with desired amount of sugar. I usually do about ⅛ cup. Very gentle mix so fruit is coated with sugar. Cover with plastic wrap and set in refrigerator. Grease a 9x13 inch loaf pan. In s bowl, combine flour, baking powder and salt. In another bowl, beat the sugar (remaining 1 cup) and butter together until light and fluffy. Add eggs, grated lemon and vanilla. Fold in dry ingredients until well combined. Batter will be thick. Pour batter into greased pan and bake for one hour in 325 degree oven or until toothpick inserted in center comes out clean. Let cool before removing from loaf pan. Wrap in plastic wrap until ready to serve. Serve at room temp with fresh fruit and whipped cream.

8 Servings

My mom used to make this dessert at family gatherings when I was growing up. Now I am carrying on that tradition. This dessert is especially good at summertime gatherings! My son, Charlie's birthday dessert request for many years! For an added festive flare for birthdays or holidays, add colored sprinkles to top with cookie crumbs. If making for a dessert over the Christmas holidays, use mint chocolate chip ice cream or peppermint ice cream and add crushed candy canes to top with cookie crumbs!

Oreo Ice Cream Dessert

1 package Oreo cookies regular or Double Stuffed
½ stick of butter, softened
½ gallon cookies and cream ice cream or vanilla bean ice cream, softened
16 oz hot fudge divided
16 oz Cool Whip, divided
Sprinkles, optional

Remove ice cream from freezer to soften a bit. In a food processor (if you don't have a food processor, place cookies in a large zip lock bag and crush with a rolling pin), blend cookies to a crumb like texture. Set aside ½ cup or so of cookie crumbs. Add rest of the cookie crumbs to a bowl and add the butter. Mix to combine. Press firmly into a 9x13 greased pan to make a crust. Place pan in freezer for 10 minutes to chill so that the ice cream layer is easier to spread. In a large bowl, mix softened ice cream and 8oz of Cool Whip. Spread mixture over chilled crust. Cover and freeze for 30 minutes. Next, spread fudge topping over ice cream. Don't fret if kind of thick and can't completely cover the ice cream layer. Smooth out as best you can. Top with remaining Cool Whip and sprinkle remaining cookie crumbs on top. Cover and freeze for at least two hours to set.

12 Servings

My mom made this ice cream pumpkin pie every Thanksgiving when I was a kid. Now I make it every Thanksgiving instead of traditional pumpkin pie. It is a family favorite!

Ice Cream Pumpkin Pie

1 - 9 inch graham cracker pie crust (use my homemade pie crust recipe!)
1 cup canned pumpkin (not pumpkin pie filling but pure pumpkin)
1 T pumpkin pie spice
1 quart vanilla bean ice cream softened
1 cup whipped cream (store bought Reddi -Wip works great!)
1/2 cup brown sugar

Put graham cracker crust in freezer to chill for fifteen minutes. Blend together pumpkin, sugar, salt and pumpkin pie spice. Fold in softened ice cream. Fill crust and place in freezer until pumpkin mixture is frozen. Cut into 8 pieces and top each slice with a dollop of Reddi-Wip whipping cream.

8 Servings

Homemade graham cracker crust is soooo much better than a store bought crust. Do not be intimidated by a homemade crust, especially a graham cracker crust.

Graham Cracker Pie Crust

9 whole graham crackers, crushed
3 T brown sugar
⅛ t salt
6 T butter

Crush graham crackers by placing in a sealed plastic bag and crushing with a rolling pin or crush in a food processor if you own one. Place graham cracker crumbs and rest of ingredients in a bowl, mix well and place in a greased 9 inch pie pan. Use lightly greased hands or back of a measuring cup to firmly press graham cracker mixture into bottom and up the sides of the pie pan. In order for crust to stay together, it needs to be firmly pressed into pie pan.

Bake crust for 10 minutes in a 350 degree oven. This step helps to set crust. Before filling the crust, let the crust cool completely.

Sweets For Your Sweets

When my mom had her 70th birthday party, we had a celebration with my three sisters and my dad at my house. We hired a chef to come to our house and cook for us one of the nights. Chef Theo was our chef and he shared this incredible chocolate mousse dessert recipe. It is such a rich and decadent dessert but super easy to make, thus the name! It can be made a day ahead of time. GF

Easy Chocolate Mousse

2 ¼ cup heavy cream
7 oz bittersweet chocolate, chopped
1 ½ t vanilla
⅛ t salt
Fresh raspberries for topping
Reddi Wip whipped cream for topping (optional)

Place mixing bowl in refrigerator to chill. Heat ½ cup of the cream in a small sauce pan until heated through. Place chopped chocolate in a bowl and pour hot cream over. Let mixture sit for one minute then whisk to smooth. Add vanilla. Remove chilled bowl from refrigerator, beat remaining one cup of cream and salt until soft peaks form. Slowly incorporate the chocolate mixture. Do not mix. Spoon mousse into a pastry bag or Ziploc bag with corner snipped. Pipe into wine glasses. Top with fresh raspberries and chill until ready to serve. If using Reddi Wip for topping, top first and then the raspberries.

4 Servings

Another great recipe from my mom! These lemon bars are the perfect dessert for a bridal/baby shower, grad parties, or a lunch/ dinner gathering in spring/summer. They freeze well too!

Lemon Bars

Crust

½ cup butter
¼ cup powdered sugar
1 cup flour
Mix above ingredients and pat into a 8 inch or 9 inch square pan. Bake in 300 degree oven for 20 minutes. Remove from oven and turn oven up to 350. Let crust cool for 15 minutes before adding the filling.

Filling

2 eggs
2 T flour
2 T lemon juice
1 cup sugar
½ t baking powder
Mix above ingredients and pour over baked and cooled crust. Bake in 350 degree oven for 20 minutes. Remove from oven and let cool before adding frosting.

Frosting

1 cups powdered sugar
1 T butter
1 T lemon juice
Milk to soften
Mix above ingredients together and start with 1 T milk to soften frosting and add more if frosting is too thick and not spreadable. Frost once the filling has cooled.

This recipe is not difficult to make but you need patience as the crust needs to cool before adding the filling. The filling needs to cool before adding the frosting. If you rush it, the bars will be soggy and won't hold their shape. I speak from experience!

12 Servings

This is a standard Christmas cookie that is super easy to make, freezes well and hopefully will become your holiday baking tradition. You can make them before Thanksgiving and freeze until Christmas time. Another Callahan family favorite and always the first to go on a Christmas cookie platter.

Peanut Blossoms

1 ¾ cup flour
1 t baking soda
½ t salt
½ cup butter, softened
¾ cup white sugar, divided
½ cup brown sugar
½ cup peanut butter
1 egg
2 T milk
1 t vanilla
48 Brach's chocolate stars

Mix flour, baking soda and salt together and set aside. In a separate bowl, mix together softened butter (not melted - room temp or a quick zap in microwave to soften a bit so easier to mix), ½ cup brown sugar, ½ cup white sugar (put other ¼ cup sugar in a bowl for rolling dough), peanut butter, egg, milk and vanilla. Once combined, add in your dry ingredients (flour, salt, baking soda). Mix together until well combined. Shape into 1 inch balls and roll in ¼ cup (may need more) of the sugar and place on ungreased cookie sheet about 2 inches apart. Place in 350 degree oven for 8 to 10 minutes or until edges of cookie are a light golden brown. Remove from oven and immediately press a chocolate star in center of each cookie. Using a spatula, gently remove cookies to a cooling rack.

Most people use chocolate Kisses for this recipe. I like to use the Brach's chocolate stars. They come unwrapped so less time consuming vs unwrapping each individual chocolate Kiss and pressing on to cookie. You can buy the Brach's chocolate stars at Walmart or on Amazon.

Makes 4 dozen

My mom has been making these for as long as I can remember. Great autumn dessert! The brown sugar frosting recipe is another option to frost these bars. Both options are delicious. I usually double the frosting as I like to spread it on thick!

Pumpkin Bars

1 cup butter
1 ⅓ cup brown sugar
1 cup canned pumpkin
1 t baking pwder
1 t cinnamon
¼ t allspice
1 t vanilla
2 eggs slightly beaten
2 cups flour
¼ t salt
¼ t baking soda
½ t ginger
¼ t nutmeg

Frosting - Option A
2 T butter
1 ½ cups powdered sugar
2 T orange juice

Brown Sugar Frosting - Option B
⅓ cup firmly packed brown sugar
1 stick butter
1 t vanilla
1 ½ cups powdered sugar
¼ t nutmeg
1 t cinnamon
2 T heavy whipping cream or more if frosting too thick

Cream butter and sugar. Add vanilla and beaten eggs. Add pumpkin and blend well. Add dry ingredients to creamed mixture. Blend until smooth. Pour into an 11x15 well greased pan. Bake in 350 degree oven for 35 minutes. Remove from oven and let cool. Mix frosting ingredients together and spread over cooled bars.

18 Servings

My sister-in-law, Laura gave me this recipe. These bars are great for nonchocolate fans. You can freeze for up to three months!

Raspberry Butter Bars

1 ½cups all - purpose flour
1 t baking soda
1 t salt
2 ½ cups quick cooking oats
¾ cup sugar
¾ cup packed brown sugar
1 cup (2 sticks) butter, melted
1 - 12 oz jar (1 ½ cups raspberry jam)
Powdered sugar, optional

Preheat oven to 325 degrees. Mix flour, baking soda and salt in a large bowl. Add oats, sugar and melted butter. Mix well. Press half of mixture into a greased 9x13 inch baking dish. Spread jam over the top. Sprinkle with remaining crumbs. Press crumbs down lightly with back of spoon. Bake for 40 to 45 minutes or until center is set and edges are golden brown and pulling away a bit from sides of pan, Let cool in pan. Cut and serve or wrap pan in plastic and then foil and freeze for up the 3 months. Sprinkle with powdered sugar when ready to serve

12 Servings

My mom used to make this pie for me every year for my birthday. Whenever the month of February rolls around, I crave this pie! It's a perfect dessert for Valentine's Day!

Mile High Strawberry Pie

1 cup sugar
2 egg whites
1 - 10 oz package frozen strawberries, halved
1 t vanilla
2 T lemon juice
Pinch of salt
1 cup whipping cream
1 - 9 inch graham cracker crust

Whip the cream until soft peaks form and chill in refrigerator. Beat egg whites until fluffy. Add frozen strawberries, sugar, vanilla and lemon juice. Beat on high speed for 20 minutes. Fold in whipped cream and scoop into a prepared graham cracker crust, preferably a homemade graham cracker crust from the recipe in this cookbook (page 129) as so much better than store bought. Place pie in freezer for at least five hours to set. When ready to serve, remove from freezer 15 minutes before serving.

8 Servings

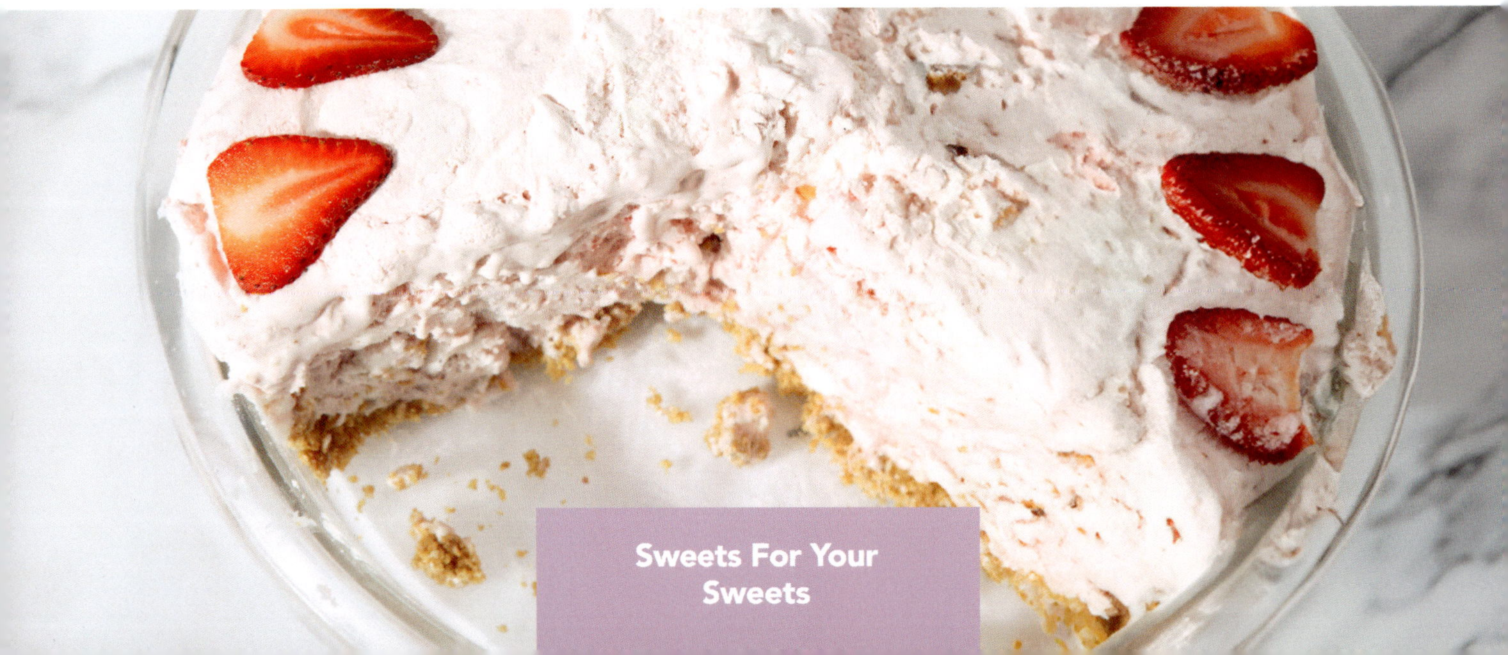

This is a family recipe from my two friends, whom are sisters, Camille and Celine. Camille and I were next door neighbors for years. All of our kids grew up together and have remained friends all these years. Such a gift!

Oatmeal Caramel Bars

32 caramels
4 T milk
1 T butter
1 cup flour
1 cup quick cooking oats
¾ cup brown sugar
½ t baking soda
¼ t salt
¾ cup butter, melted
1 cup semi sweet chocolate chips

Preheat oven to 350 degrees. In a saucepan on low heat add caramels, milk and butter. Stir until caramels are melted and mixture is well combined. In a mixing bowl, combine flour, oats, brown sugar, baking soda, salt and melted butter. Press half of the oat mixture into a greased 9x13 inch pan. Bake in oven for 10 minutes. Remove from oven and sprinkle with one cup chocolate chips. Pour caramel mixture over chocolate chips. Sprinkle remaining oat mixture over top. Bake 15 minutes or until center is set and sides are slightly pulling away from pan. Remove from oven and let cool before cutting into bars.

12 Servings

I got this recipe from the Minneapolis Star Tribune Taste section in 1990's and have been making them every year for the holidays. I love the salty crunch combined with the sweetness of the chocolate and the chewiness of the caramel. It is my go-to for Christmas cookie exchanges too, as so pretty on a platter and everyone loves them!

Triple Dipped Pretzels

1 bag of caramels
2 T milk
10 oz pretzel rods
20 oz almond bark
¼ cup semisweet chocolate chips
Sprinkles (optional)

Place caramels in a microwave-safe bowl. Add milk. Microwave on high for about 3 minutes or until caramels are melted, stirring after each minute. Break pretzel rods in half and dip broken ends into melted caramels, leaving about an inch or so uncovered. Shake off excess and allow to set on a well greased baking sheet. Greasing your baking sheet is important. I grease with softened butter. If not well greased, caramel dipped pretzels will stick to pan and will break when trying to pry off of pan.

Melt almond bark in microwave per package instructions. Dip caramel coated pretzels into the melted almond bark leaving about an inch uncovered. Allow to set a second time on the well greased baking sheet. If using sprinkles, shake sprinkles onto pretzels right after they are dipped in the almond bark. Skip next section if using sprinkles.

Microwave chocolate chips until melted stirring every 30 seconds so chocolate doesn't burn. Move pretzels so they are touching on the baking sheet. Drizzle chocolate over pretzels (I dip a fork into melted chocolate and then drizzle over pretzels). Allow to set.

Makes 4 dozen

Family Thanksgiving celebration in my hometown, Dubuque, Iowa.

Cherished memory of Christmas Day at my mom's. Her last time hosting at age 91!

Happy Holidays!

Thanksgiving and Christmas are stressful times on parents. We all put so much pressure on ourselves to make the holidays special. This chapter in my cookbook is going to lessen the stress on you over the holidays. Just like most of the recipes in this cookbook, it's all about prepping food ahead of time so when guests arrive, you are not stuck in the kitchen completely stressed, distracted and intimidated. You will want to mingle with your guests and take in the special time and be in the moment!

The brunches and dessert recipes I use for the holidays are in the brunch and dessert section of this cookbook. In the Happy Holidays chapter of this cookbook, I am going to share how I prepare my turkey for Thanksgiving and the sides I make. I stick to the same sides and how I prep my turkey for Thanksgiving year after year. Yes, you could say I am a creature of habit but I like to go with what I know works well and dishes I know everyone loves. Some of these sides I make for Thanksgiving, I have been making since the early 1990's, before I had kids!

Many Christmases were spent in Iowa visiting my family and Charlie's family. My mom hosted Christmas Day for years up until she was 91! When we are home in Minnesota for the holidays, for Christmas Eve, I make either soup and sandwiches or we feast on a bunch of apps. On Christmas Day, we step it up in the fancy department with beef tenderloin, twice baked potatoes, side dishes, a salad and of course, dessert.

Try these recipes and I promise you will be less intimidated by holiday menus and you will be creating wonderful memories for your family. You're welcome and Happy Holidays!

Turkey Made Easy

Unlike the cover, my turkey has never started on fire! Turkey is actually easier than you think to cook. It feels intimidating because it is such a large bird but with an instant read thermometer, it is really difficult to screw up cooking a turkey, especially if you brine it!

I always buy a frozen turkey in early November. I stick it in my downstairs freezer until I am ready to thaw it out. 4 lbs of frozen turkey meat thaws per day so do the math. The day before turkey day, I rinse my thawed turkey. Remove the giblets and neck and toss in garbage. I brine my turkey (brining makes for a super succulent turkey). I do a wet brine and I buy my brine at William Sonoma. I place in a big roasting pan with high sides. I add the brine and water per directions on label of the brine mixture I bought. The directions for the brine are super straight forward. Just be sure to flip your bird once half way through brining time. After brined, rinse your turkey really well as you want to remove all traces of salt. Pat dry. Rub soft melted butter underneath the skin of the turkey and in the cavity. I put sprigs of thyme and rosemary and chopped onions in cavity of bird for added flavor. I put some chicken broth in bottom of pan. Just enough to cover length of pan as the juices from the turkey will drip into pan and you will baste with that.

Preheat oven to 450 degrees. Roast for 25 minutes then baste and continue roasting until skin turns a light golden brown. Reduce oven to 325 and continue roasting about 1 hour and 45 minutes for a 12 pound turkey (cooking times will vary depending on your oven). Also, brined turkeys cook faster. Continue basting every 30 or so minutes. Check with instant read thermometer in turkey breast. Should be 165 degrees. Remove turkey from oven and cover with foil to keep warm once turkey is done. I found that homemade gravy from a brined turkey is too salty so I buy my gravy at William Sonoma. Shhh...

Once you make this sweet potato dish for Thanksgiving, you will never try another sweet potato recipe again. This will be your go-to every year and your family and friends will thank you for it. My sister, Carol gave me this recipe when my kids were little and I have been making it every year for Thanksgiving. When my daughter, Molly is at her in-law's house in Chicago for Thanksgiving, they always ask her to bring this dish as they now love it too! GF

Apples With Sweet Potatoes & Marshmallow Casserole

4 lbs sweet potatoes cut into ⅓ inch thick rounds
1 cup chopped pecans, optional
1 cup raisins, optional
1 cup brown sugar
1 ¼ t cinnamon
1 ½ cups mini marshmallows
6 Granny Smith apples peeled and cut into ⅓ inch slices
1 ¼ sticks butter, melted

Preheat oven to 400 degree. Toss potatoes, pecans, raisins, brown sugar and cinnamon in large bowl, mixing well to coat potatoes. Place ½ apples in a well greased 9x13 dish. Arrange ½ of sweet potatoes over apples. Drizzle with ½ melted butter and repeat layers. Drizzle with remaining butter. Place in oven for 1 hour and 45 minutes. Remove from oven and sprinkle marshmallows over potato mixture and broil for one minute.

12 Servings

This broccoli side dish is my mom's recipe. She made it all the time for Thanksgiving dinner. Now I do the same and you can too! It pairs so well with almost any fall/winter entrée so don't just save it for the holidays. Easy, delicious and double this recipe as it goes fast!

Broccoli Corn Bake

1 - 10 oz package frozen chopped broccoli
1 - 16 oz can creamed corn
½ cup cracker crumbs (I use Ritz)
1 egg beaten
4 T butter, melted
1 T onion flakes
1 t salt
⅛ t pepper

Combine broccoli with corn and ¼ cup of bread crumbs. Add onion, 2 T of melted butter, salt and pepper. Put in greased 2 quart casserole dish. Sprinkle remaining crumbs on top and drizzle remaining 2 T of butter on top. Bake uncovered at 350 degrees for 30 – 35 minutes. Skip cracker topping for GF or use GF crackers.

4 Servings

Back in 1993, my mom gave me a subscription to the Bon Appetit magazine and their November issue had this cranberry dish in it. I have been making this for Thanksgiving every year I have hosted (unless we were celebrating Thanksgiving in Iowa where my husband and I are from). Never have I deviated from this recipe as there is literally nothing to change. It's the perfect blend of tangy and sweet AND you can make it three days ahead of time. GF

Cranberry Salad

1 cup frozen cranberry juice cocktail, concentrate, thawed
⅓ cup sugar
1 - 12 oz package fresh cranberries, rinsed and drained
½ cup dried cranberries
3 T orange marmalade (I have used apricot preserves if could not find orange marmalade)
2 T fresh orange juice
2 t grated orange peel
¼ t ground all spice

Combine cranberry juice concentrate and sugar in medium size saucepan. Bring to a boil over high heat, stirring until sugar dissolves. Add fresh and dried cranberries to pan. Cook until dried cranberries begin to soften and fresh berries begin to pop. Stir often for 6 to 7 minutes. Remove from heat and stir in orange marmalade, orange juice, orange peel and allspice. Cool completely. Place in a pretty glass/crystal bowl, cover and chill until cold.

8 Servings

I would be remiss if I did not put my grandma's apricot salad recipe in this cookbook. It is a jello salad and think 1970's vibes. My grandma, then my mom and now my sisters and I make this salad every Thanksgiving as a nod to tradition. Apricot jello is difficult to find so I usually substitute peach jello. GF

Great Grandma's Apricot Salad

1 - 3 oz package apricot (or peach) jello
¾ cup sugar
1 - 8 oz can crushed pineapple
8 oz cream cheese, softened
8 oz Cool Whip

Mix jello and crushed pineapple in a saucepan. Bring to a boil and then set aside and cool. Once mixture is cooled, mix in softened cream cheese and then gently fold in the Cool Whip. Place in a glass or crystal bowl, chill to set.

This traditional stuffing recipe is a winner. The sausage, sage, thyme and red peppers make this dish savory and so pretty.

Stuffing Stuffing

1 pound unseasoned bread cubes. (I use Brownberry. Too intimidating to make your own).
1 pound pork sausage
¾ cup butter
3 celery stalks, chopped
1 large onion, chopped
1 large red pepper, chopped
2 t minced garlic
2 t poultry seasoning
1 t minced fresh thyme or ¼ t dried
1 ½ t chopped fresh sage or 1/3 t dried
1 ¼ cup chicken stock divided
2 eggs, beaten
½ cup chopped fresh parsley
Pepper to taste

Preheat oven to 375 degrees. Cook sausage in heavy skillet over medium high heat until cooked through and no longer pink. Using a slotted spoon, transfer pork into a large bowl. Add butter to any drippings. Melt over medium high heat. Add celery, onions, bell pepper, and seasonings to skillet and saute for 10 minutes, adding garlic last minute of cooking time. Add mixture to sausage then mix in bread cubes. Add 1 cup chicken stock to skillet and scape up any browned bits. Pour over the stuffing. Add eggs and parsley and mix well.

Place in a greased 9x13 pan and bake for 25 to 30 minutes. Add remaining chicken stock to stuffing half way through baking time. Once stuffing is done, add some of your turkey drippings to the stuffing. Cover with foil to keep warm until ready to serve.

12 Servings

Ina Garten, another inspirational cook for me, has a cookbook titled "Make It Ahead." One of her recipes is a make ahead mashed potato dish. My version was inspired by Ina's mashed potato recipe. It's so important to be able to make dishes ahead of time. Such a time and stress saver! GF

Make Ahead Mashed Potatoes

3 pounds Yukon Gold potatoes, peel and cut into medium sized even chunks
½ T salt
1 - 5.2 oz Boursin Garlic & Fine Herbs cheese
4 T butter, softened
1 ½ cups sour cream
½ cup heavy whipping cream
¾ cup grated parmesan cheese
Salt and Pepper to taste

Preheat oven to 375 unless making it ahead. Place potatoes in heavy stockpot. Fill with enough water until potatoes are covered. On high heat, bring water and potatoes in pot to a boil, then reduce to just above a simmer and cook for 25 minutes. Once a dinner knife can be easily inserted into a potato, they are done. Drain potatoes using a colander and let potatoes sit in colander for a few minutes to make sure no water is dripping off the potatoes. Add the cheese, butter, sour cream and heavy whipping cream. Using a potato masher, mash up potatoes incorporating ingredients as you go. Be careful not to overmix potatoes as they will get gummy. Once potatoes are mashed and other ingredients are mixed in, add salt and pepper as needed and place potatoes in a 9x13 inch pan. Sprinkle the parmesan cheese. At this point, if you are making these potatoes ahead of time, cover in plastic wrap or foil and place in refrigerator one, two or three days ahead of time. Bake in a 375 degree oven for 45 minutes.

12 Servings

That's A Wrap!

The ones who inspire me to make great meals.

Index

Entrees (Cont.)

Sides

Desserts

A special thanks to Brien Spanier and my husband, Charlie for the eye catching cover design. Thank you to Lisa Valley for all of your help and guidance with the food styling and photography. Thank you to Emily Lanctot for the wonderful layout and for your patience as we figured this thing out. You all brought this cookbook to life and were a joy to work with!